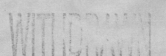

Collins Children's Picture Atlas
Collins
An imprint of HarperCollins Publishers
Westerhill Road
Bishopbriggs
Glasgow
G64 2QT

© HarperCollins Publishers Ltd 2012
Maps © CollinsBartholomew Ltd 2012

First published as Collins Children's Pictorial Atlas 2007
Reprinted 2009, 2011
This edition 2012
ISBN 978-0-00-747944-3
Imp 001   ९।२
Collins ® is a registered trademark of
HarperCollins Publishers Ltd

British Library Cataloguing in Publication Data
A catalogue record for this book is available from the British Library.

Printed and bound in China

All mapping in this atlas is generated from CollinsBartholomew digital
databases. CollinsBartholomew, the UK's leading independent
geographical information supplier, can provide a digital, custom, and
premium mapping service to a variety of markets.
For further information:
Tel: +44 (0) 208 307 4515
e-mail: collinsbartholomew@harpercollins.co.uk
Visit our websites at:
www.collinseducation.com
www.collinsbartholomew.com
www.collinsmaps.com

Collins

Children's
PICTURE ATLAS

Collins

Contents

How to use the atlas

Take a journey around the world with this atlas. It is divided up into continents, regions and countries. Each map is full of small picture symbols which will introduce you to the lifestyle of people, wildlife and interesting places found in far off lands.

World maps

The introductory pages show maps of the whole world and from these you can find the regions with the most interesting features. You can find out more about these by searching through the continents and regions mapped in the rest of the atlas. At the bottom of each World page is a list of symbols used on pages within the atlas. Try to find the countries where the symbols are shown then look at the other interesting features found in that country.

Below the world map each 'Did you know? lists some fascinating facts and statistics.

- Only 12 people have ever walked on the moon.
- It takes 45 minutes to put on a space suit.
- A spacecraft takes 3 days to travel from earth to the moon.

World

The world is full of interesting places. Many countries have famous buildings like castles, churches and palaces and some of these are named on the map.

Arctic

Seattle Space Needle

NORTH AMERICA

Statue of Liberty

Edinburgh Castle

EUROPE

Eiffel Tower

Colosseum

Kennedy Space Center

Mexican pyramid

Atlantic

Ocean

Pacific

Ocean

SOUTH AMERICA

Statue de Jesus

Did you know?

- Only 12 people have ever walked on the moon.
- It takes 45 minutes to put on a space suit.
- A spacecraft takes 3 days to travel from earth to the moon.

Did you know?

- The Eiffel tower is over 300 metres (984 feet) high.
- There are 1660 steps from the foot of the tower to the top.
- More than 2½ million rivets hold the tower together.
- In summer, the tower is 15 centimetres (6 inches) taller because of the warmer weather.

Look through the maps in this atlas to find the other places shown below.
▼

Arc de Triomphe

Golden Temple, Amritsar

terracotta soldier

Dome of the Rock

vi

Maps of each continent

How well do you know the flags of the world? Turn to the map of a continent and every flag will be shown beside its country. In addition all the statistics about the continent are listed. These include its highest mountain, longest river, biggest country and much more.

On every spread of a continent there is also a short activity which relates to the information shown on the map.

Atlanta

New Orleans

Miami

Havana

Gulf of exico

ST KITTS AND NEVIS

ANTIGUA AND BARBUDA

THE BAHAMAS
Nassau

DOMINICA

San Juan

DOMINICAN REPUBLIC

CUBA

HAITI Port-au-Prince

Santo Domingo

PUERTO RICO (USA)

BARBADOS

JAMAICA
Kingston

Caribbean Sea

BELIZE

TEMALA
la City

Belmopan

HONDURAS
Tegucigalpa

ST LUCIA

GRENADA

Maps of regions and countries

Imagine you have just arrived in a new country. What will it be like? What do you want to do or see here?

The symbols placed on the countries can help you to decide. Look at the symbols in the neighbouring countries and plan a journey right across the region. There is so much to see and do.

Watch a Sumo wrestling match! Take a train journey!

Go walking in the mountains! See lots of animals!

Find out more from the facts placed around the maps.

It's a fact
The giant panda has lived in bamboo forests for several million years. Each year a panda can eat 5 tonnes of bamboo. There are only about 1600 left in the wild.

It's a fact
Ice hockey is one of Canada's most popular sports. It was first played in 1788 when some schoolboys tried to play the Irish game 'hurley' on ice. In Canada today there are over 500 000 players.

Try the activity found at the bottom of each map.

This will let you know just how much you have learnt from the map. All the answers are listed at the back of the atlas.

Try this!
China has many different animals. Look at the map and find

The big furry animal who loves to eat bamboo.

Many sports are played in Japan

Can you name 2 of these?

Try this!
Canada has many different animals and birds. Look at the map and find

4 types of bird
2 types of dog
3 furry wild animals

Where have you been?

You may like to see what other children think of the places they have visited or lived in. On pages 48–51 you can read some of the comments we have gathered from children. Have you been to the same places? What comment would you make about the places you have visited?

Kenya
We were in a big car and saw elephants and lions. I liked the lions but they had big teeth. It was very dusty and hot.
Katie

USA
I like Universal Studio because it has fantastic rides. I would give it a ten out of ten.
Sam

Index

You may know the name of a place you would like to visit but can't find the map it appears on. Turn to the index and find the name. The index will tell you which page in the atlas to turn to and where the place is on the map.

World

The world is full of interesting places. Many countries have famous buildings like castles, churches and palaces and some of these are named on the map.

A r c t i c

NORTH AMERICA

Seattle Space Needle

Statue of Liberty

Kennedy Space Center

Mexican pyramid

Edinburgh Castle

EUROPE

Eiffel Tower

Colosseum

Atlantic

Ocean

Pacific

Ocean

SOUTH AMERICA

Statue de Jesus

Did you know?

- Only 12 people have ever walked on the moon.
- It takes 45 minutes to put on a space suit.
- A spacecraft takes 3 days to travel from earth to the moon.

Did you know?

- The Eiffel tower is over 300 metres (984 feet) high.
- There are 1660 steps from the foot of the tower to the top.
- More than 2½ million rivets hold the tower together.
- In summer, the tower is 15 centimetres (6 inches) taller because of the warmer weather.

Look through the maps in this atlas to find the other places shown below.
▼

Arc de Triomphe

Golden Temple, Amritsar

terracotta soldier

Dome of the Rock

Interesting places

a n

Kremlin

ASIA

Great Wall of China

Sphinx

Taj Mahal

Pacific

Ocean

C A

Indian

Ocean

Did you know?

• The Great Wall of China is the
longest wall in the world.
• It winds up and down mountains
and across fields and deserts.
• The wall is as tall as 2 double
decker buses

OCEANIA

u house

Sydney Opera House

Chilean chapel

Big Ben

Berber architecture

Angkor Wat

World

Animals and birds live all over the world. Each have their favourite places to live. This may depend on the climate and vegetation of the country in which they are found.

Arcti

Highland cattle

EURO

puffin

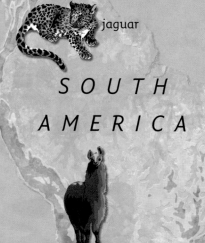
caribou

NORTH
AMERICA

bobcat

bald eagle

gila monster

camel

Atlantic

Ocean

pygmy hippopotamus

jaguar

Pacific

Ocean

SOUTH
AMERICA

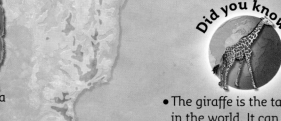
alpaca

Did you know?

- Penguins are birds that cannot fly.
- They have waterproof feathers and are expert swimmers.
- The smallest penguin is called a Fairy Penguin.

Did you know?

- The giraffe is the tallest animal in the world. It can grow to more than 5 metres (16 feet) tall.
- A giraffe can live without water for longer than a camel. It can run faster than a horse.
- A giraffe can clean its ears with its very long tongue.

Look through the maps in this atlas to find the other animals and birds shown below.

▼

penguins

koala

poison arrow
frog

spiny
anteater

peacock

Animals and Birds

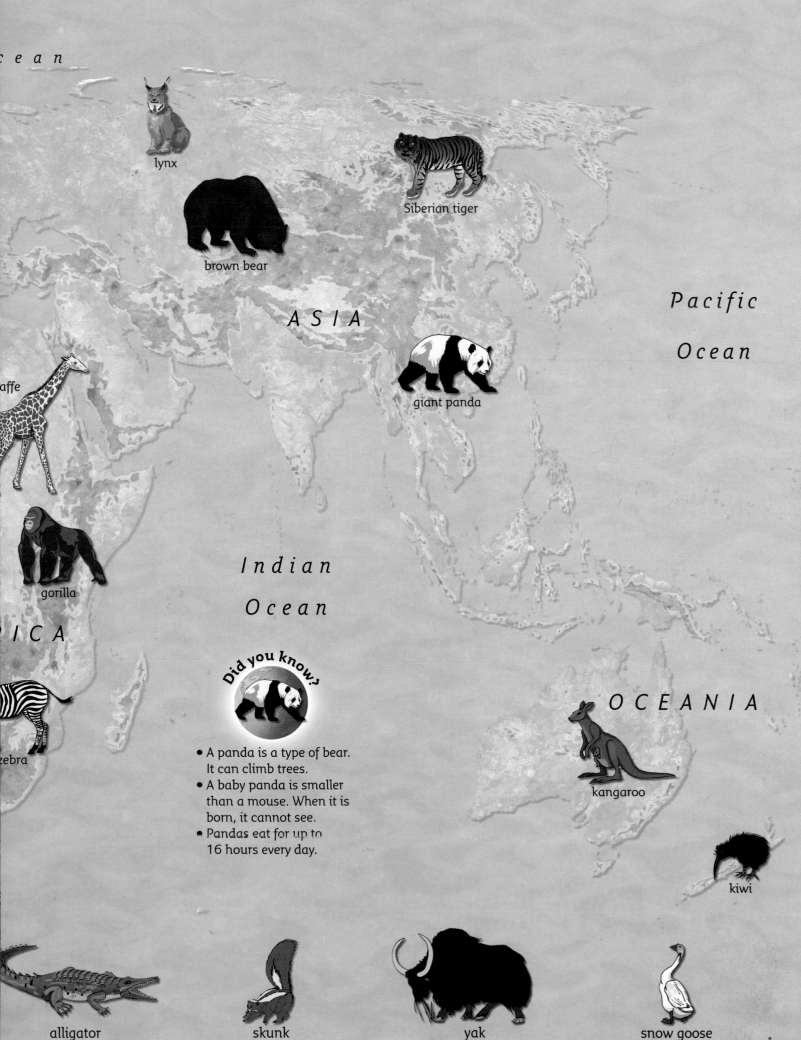

ocean

lynx

brown bear

Siberian tiger

Pacific

Ocean

A S I A

giant panda

affe

gorilla

I n d i a n

O c e a n

PICA

zebra

Did you know?

- A panda is a type of bear. It can climb trees.
- A baby panda is smaller than a mouse. When it is born, it cannot see.
- Pandas eat for up to 16 hours every day.

O C E A N I A

kangaroo

kiwi

alligator

skunk

yak

snow goose

World

Different types of food are grown and eaten all over the world. This map of the world shows where some of our favourite foods are grown.

A r c t i c

NORTH AMERICA

apples

cranberries

peanuts

hamburgers

cheese

EUROPE

pizza

dates

Atlantic

Ocean

Pacific

Ocean

oranges

bananas

SOUTH AMERICA

Did you know?

- Apples can be all shades of red, green or yellow.
- One apple tree can produce 400 apples every year.
- Apples can be as small as a cherry, or as large as a grapefruit.

grapes

Did you know?

- A coconut can float on the water.
- Coconuts are grown in more than 90 countries of the world.
- You can drink coconut juice. It is the liquid found inside a coconut.

Look through the maps in this atlas to find the other foods shown below.

▼

tortilla

pumpkin pie

croissants

almonds

Food and Drink

a n

atoes

wheat

kebabs

ASIA

Pacific

Ocean

bowl of rice

pineapples

C A

tea

Indian

Ocean

coconuts

Did you know?

- Over half the people in the world eat rice every day.
- In China the word for rice is the same as the word for food.
- Rice is a type of grass. It is one of the oldest plants in the world.

seafood

OCEANIA

pes

kiwi fruit

spaghetti

olives

wheat

sardines

World

People play sport all over the world. Popular sports, like football, are played in almost every country. Different sports are shown on the map.

Arctic

NORTH AMERICA

snow boarding

ice hockey

American football

football

cricket

EUROPE

bull fighting

rugb...

footba...

Atlantic Ocean

Pacific Ocean

SOUTH AMERICA

surfing

motor racing

football

polo

Did you know?

- There are different types of football, such as American football, Australian football and Gaelic football.
- Blind people use a ball filled with ball bearings, so that they can hear it.
- Bright orange footballs are used when it is snowy.

Did you know?

- Hockey can be played on ice, on a field or under the water.
- A hockey stick can be shaped like a J or an L.
- Hockey was played in Egypt thousands of years ago.

Look through the maps in this atlas to find the other sports and activities shown below.
▼

curling

baseball

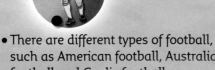
skiing

yachting

Sports and Activities

a n

ASIA

chess

karate

Pacific

Ocean

hockey

cricket

ICA

Indian

Ocean

Did you know?

- To surf you stand or lie on a board and float on the waves of the sea.
- Dolphins and whales like to surf the waves.
- The word surf can also mean to look at different pages of the World Wide Web on a computer.

Australian football

OCEANIA

tennis

surfing

rugby

ket

sumo wrestling

lacrosse

scuba diving

gymnastics

World

Seas and oceans cover two thirds of the earth's surface. The rest is land. The land is divided up into seven large masses of land known as continents.

Greenland

Arctic

Mount McKinley

Rocky Mountains

NORTH
AMERICA

R. Missouri

R. Mississippi

Yosemite Falls

Niagara Falls

EURO

Atlas Mountains

Saha
Dese

The map shows some of the largest features on each continent.

Caribbean Sea

Atlantic

Ocean

Pacific

Ocean

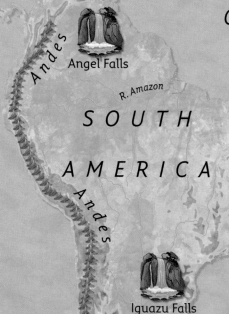
Andes
Angel Falls

R. Amazon

SOUTH
AMERICA

Andes

Iguazu Falls

Aconcagua

Did you know?

- Deserts cover a third of the world's surface.
- The Sahara is the world's largest desert.
- The highest sand dunes are found in Algeria.
- The highest temperatures in the world occur in the Sahara, however the nights can be very cold.

Did you know?

- The world's highest mountain range is Himalaya.
- Mount Everest is the highest peak at 8848 metres (29 029 feet).
- It was once known as Peak 15.
- Mount Everest was formed about 60 million years ago.
- Mount Everest was named after Sir George Everest the British surveyor-general of India.

M
D

A global view of each continent is shown here. ▶

North America lies between the Atlantic and Pacific Oceans.

South America stretches from the Caribbean Sea towards the South Pole.

Europe is one of the smallest continents.

Natural Features

Ural Mountains

R. Ob'

R. Volga

Caucasus

Black Sea

El'brus

Caspian Sea

...nean Sea

R. Nile

Arabian Peninsula

S i b e r i a

A S I A

Kunlun Shan

H i m a l a y a

R. Ganges

Mount Everest

Gobi Desert

Chang Jiang

Pacific Ocean

Arabian Sea

Bay of Bengal

South China Sea

I C A

R. Congo

Kilimanjaro

...ria Falls

...alahari Desert

Tugela Falls

I n d i a n   O c e a n

Borneo

Puncak Jaya

New Guinea

Did you know?

- Angel Falls, in Venezuela, is the world's highest waterfall at 979 metres (3212 feet).
- Victoria Falls, on the Zambezi river between Zambia and Zimbabwe, is the largest. It is 1.7 kilometres (1 mile) wide and 128 metres (420 feet) high.
- Niagara Falls is the most powerful falls in North America.

Great Sandy Desert

Great Victoria Desert

O C E A N I A

...ica is almost equally balanced ... either side of the Equator.

Asia is the largest continent.

Oceania is made up of Australia and many small islands.

Antarctica encircles the South Pole.

World

Continents are divided up into many different countries. There are over 190 countries in the world. Lines are drawn on the map to show where two countries meet. These are known as international boundaries.

GREENLAND
(Denmark)

U.S.A.

C A N A D A

More detailed map
Europe can be four
pages 22-29

UNITED STATES
OF AMERICA

Azores
(Portugal)

TUN

MOROCCO

ALGERIA   LI

WESTERN
SAHARA

THE
BAHAMAS

MEXICO

CUBA

DOMINICAN
HAITI REP.

MAURITANIA

MALI NIGER

Mexico City ○
is the largest city
in North America GUATEMALA

BELIZE   JAMAICA

HONDURAS

PUERTO
RICO
(USA)

CAPE VERDE   SENEGAL

THE GAMBIA

GUINEA-BISSAU

BURKINA

EL SALVADOR   NICARAGUA

GUINEA

BENIN
TOGO
GHANA

NIGERIA

This map also shows
the largest city in
each continent. ○

COSTA RICA

PANAMA

VENEZUELA

TRINIDAD
& TOBAGO

GUYANA

SIERRA
LEONE

CÔTE
D'IVOIRE

LIBERIA

COLOMBIA

SURINAME
FRENCH
GUIANA

CAMEROON
EQUITORIAL
GUINEA

Galapagos Is
(Ecuador)

ECUADOR

GABON

P
E
R
U

B R A Z I L

C
O

AN

Did you know?

When it is 12 noon in New York the time is
• 5 pm in London
• 3 am in Sydney
• 8 pm in Moscow
• Midnight in Bangkok
• 9 am in Los Angeles

BOLIVIA

C
H
I
L
E

PARAGUAY

A
R
G
E
N
T
I
N
A

URUGUAY

Sao Paulo ○
is the largest city in
South America

NA

Did you know?

These countries have two capital cities.
• The Netherlands has The Hague
  and Amsterdam
• Malaysia has Kuala Lumpur
  and Putrajaya
• Bolivia has La Paz and Sucre
• South Africa has Pretoria
  and Cape Town
• Myanmar has Naypyidaw
  and Yangon

The flags of the eight largest countries in
the world are shown below. Look through
the rest of the atlas to find out more
interesting facts about life in these countries.

Falkland Islands
(UK)

South Georgia
(UK)

▼   Russian Federation

Canada

China

United States of America

17 075 400 square kilometres
6 592 849 square miles

9 984 670 square kilometres
3 855 103 square miles

9 620 671 square kilometres
3 714 562 square miles

9 826 635 square kilometre
3 794 085 square miles

Countries and Cities

RUSSIAN FEDERATION

○ **Moscow**
is the largest city
in Europe

KAZAKHSTAN

MONGOLIA

GEORGIA
ARMENIA AZERBAIJAN
UZBEKISTAN
KYRGYZSTAN

TURKEY
TURKMENISTAN
TAJIKISTAN

N. KOREA

JAPAN

RUS
SYRIA
EBANON
IRAQ
AFGHAN-
ISTAN
CHINA
S. KOREA
○ **Tokyo**
is the largest city
in Asia

ISRAEL
JORDAN
KUWAIT
IRAN
PAKISTAN

○airo
e largest
in Africa

SAUDI
BAHRAIN
QATAR
NEPAL
BHUTAN

GYPT
UNITED ARAB
EMIRATES
INDIA
BANGLA-
DESH

ARABIA OMAN
MYANMAR
(BURMA)
LAOS
VIETNAM

ERITREA **YEMEN**
THAILAND
PHILIPPINES

*Northern
Mariana Is.
(USA)*

DAN
DJIBOUTI
CAMBODIA
**MARSHALL
ISLANDS**

OUTH
UDAN
ETHIOPIA
SOMALIA
SRI
LANKA
PALAU
**FED. STATES OF
MICRONESIA**

UGANDA
MALDIVES
BRUNEI

ATIC
KENYA
MALAYSIA

RWANDA
SINGAPORE
NAURU

BURUNDI
SEYCHELLES
I N D O N E S I A
**PAPUA
NEW
GUINEA**

TANZANIA

EAST
TIMOR
**SOLOMON
ISLANDS**

MALAWI
COMOROS

BIA
MAURITIUS
VANUATU

ABWE
FIJI

ANA
MADAGASCAR
*New
Caledonia
(France)*

SWAZILAND
A U S T R A L I A

ESOTHO

F
A

Did you know?

The time taken to fly between
• Los Angeles and Sydney is 14½ hours
• London and Tokyo is 12½ hours
• Paris and New York is 8½ hours
• Bangkok and Perth is 6¾ hours

○ **Sydney**
is the largest city
in Oceania

**NEW
ZEALAND**

*Îles Kerguélen
(France)*

Brazil	Australia	India	Argentina
514 879 square kilometres	7 692 024 square kilometres	3 064 989 square kilometres	2 766 889 square kilometres
3 287 613 square miles	2 969 907 square miles	1 183 364 square miles	1 068 302 square miles

North America

North America is the largest continent in the western hemisphere. It is surrounded by great oceans: the Arctic to the north, the Pacific to the west and the Atlantic to the east. The countries of North America are a mixture of the large nations of Canada, USA and Mexico in the north and the tiny Caribbean island nations in the south. It is joined to South America by the narrow strip of land known as the isthmus of Panama.

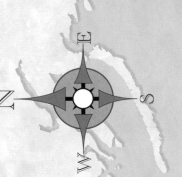

People facts

- Population: 517 000 000
- Country with most people:
  United States of America 298 213 000
- City with most people:
  Mexico City 19 013 000

Geography facts

- Area: 24 680 331 square kilometres
  (9 529 129 square miles)
- Largest country: Canada
  9 984 670 square kilometres
  (3 855 103 square miles)
- Longest river: Mississippi-Missouri
  5969 kilometres (3709 miles)
- Highest mountain: Mount McKinley
  6194 metres (20 321 feet)
- Largest lake: Lake Superior
  82 100 square kilometres
  (31 698 square miles)
- Largest island: Greenland
  2 175 600 square kilometres
  (840 004 square miles)

⑦

⑥

⑤

Arctic Ocean

Bering Sea

ALASKA
U.S.A.
▲ Mount
  McKinley
○ **Anchorage**

GREENLAND
(Denmark)

□
Nuuk

Baffin Bay

Baffin Island

Hudson Bay

Rock

Atlantic Ocean

ANTIGUA AND BARBUDA

DOMINICA

BARBADOS

ST KITTS AND NEVIS

GRENADA

San Juan

PUERTO RICO (USA)

ST LUCIA

ST VINCENT AND THE GRENADINES

Bermuda (UK)

DOMINICAN REPUBLIC

Santo Domingo

THE BAHAMAS

Nassau

HAITI

Port-au-Prince

Kingston

CUBA

JAMAICA

Caribbean Sea

SOUTH AMERICA

Boston

New York

Washington D.C.

Ottawa

Toronto

Detroit

Atlanta

St Louis

Chicago

Minneapolis

Denver

Phoenix

San Francisco

Los Angeles

Seattle

Lake Superior

R. Mississippi

R. Missouri

Miami

New Orleans

Gulf of Mexico

Havana

UNITED STATES OF AMERICA

Dallas

Houston

Monterrey

Guadalajara

MEXICO

Mexico City

Puebla

BELIZE

Belmopan

Tegucigalpa

HONDURAS

GUATEMALA

Guatemala City

San Salvador

EL SALVADOR

Managua

NICARAGUA

San José

COSTA RICA

Panama City

PANAMA

Pacific Ocean

...ountains

Did you know?

• The United States has over 250 000 rivers.

• There are over 10 000 glaciers on Baffin Island.

• The world's smallest volcano is in Puebla, Mexico.

• Belize's barrier reef at 285 kilometres (180 miles) is the longest in the western hemisphere.

• Some of the world's oldest rocks are found on the west coast of Greenland.

• 2 million caribou live in Canada.

Try this!

Unscramble these letters to find an island name.

Clue: It is the largest island in North America.

G L D E A N R E N

Answers at the back of the atlas.

Ⓐ   Ⓑ   Ⓒ   Ⓓ

①   ②   ③

3

Canada

⑤

N
W · E
S

Arctic Ocean

U.S.A.
ALASKA

polar bear

R. Yukon

Mount McKinley

caribou

ice breaker ship

Arctic hare

Arctic terns

④ volcanoes

walrus

brown bear

musk ox

husky dog

Gulf of Alaska

Mount Logan

wolves

Rocky

Pacific Ocean

forest

lumberjack

Arctic fox

moose

③

C A N

Mount Waddington

skiing

oil

killer whale

Mountains

Vancouver

ice hockey

blueberries

② port

Calgary

Canadian Pacific Railway

bobcat

wheat growing

Winnipeg

lacro

Canada is a huge country but it is not crowded.
The far north of the country is in the Arctic region
and is almost empty. Further south there are pine
forests and in the west are the Rocky Mountains.

UNITED STATE
OF AMERICA

①

Ⓐ

Ⓑ

Ⓒ

polar bear

G r e e n l a n d
(Denmark)

seal

igloo

Inuit people

...shing

ptarmigan

Canadian
goose

Nuuk
(Godthåb)

kayak

snowy owl

beluga whale

D   **A**

d s o n
a y

maple leaf

Newfoundland dog

A t l a n t i c
O c e a n

...eaver

maple syrup

lobster

timber

...ing

apples

Ottawa church

Montreal

Quebec

apples

R. St Lawrence

Lake Huron

Ottawa
cranberries

Toronto
Lake Ontario

Lake Erie

Niagara
Falls

D

E

Did you know?
- Canada has the world's longest coastline – 202 000 kilometres (125 517 miles).
- The Arctic hare has huge feet which help it to run on top of the snow.
- Canadians consume more macaroni and cheese than any other nation on earth.

What am I?
- I grow on a tree at the end of a twig.
- I am the national emblem of Canada.
- I can be seen as a bright red symbol on my country's national flag.
- Canadians eat the syrup which is taken from the trunk of my tree.

What am I?

Try this!
Canada has many different animals and birds. Look at the map and find

4 types of bird
2 types of dog
3 furry wild animals

Answers at the back of the atlas.

It's a fact
Ice hockey is one of Canada's most popular sports. It was first played in 1788 when some schoolboys tried to play the Irish game 'hurley' on ice. In Canada today there are over 500 000 players.

5

United States of America

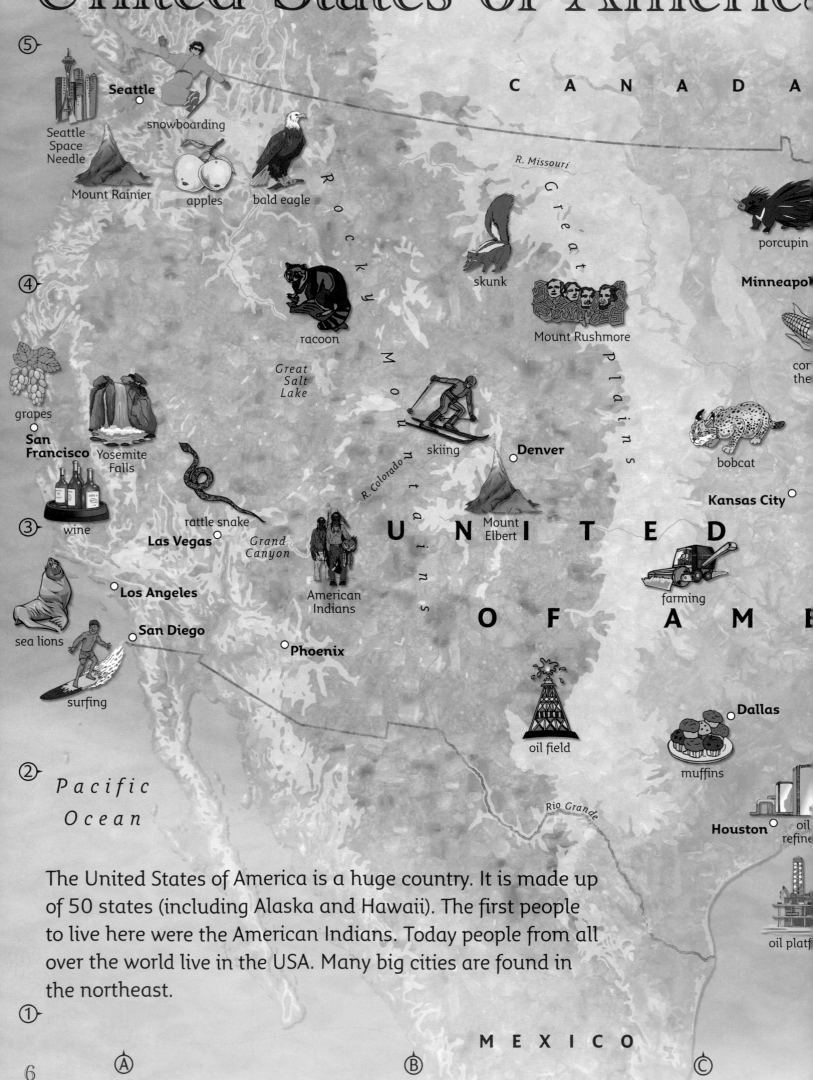

⑤

Seattle

snowboarding

Seattle Space Needle

Mount Rainier

apples

bald eagle

CANADA

R. Missouri

Great Plains

porcupine

skunk

Mount Rushmore

Minneapolis

④

racoon

Great Salt Lake

corn the

grapes

San Francisco

Yosemite Falls

skiing

Denver

bobcat

wine

③

rattle snake

R. Colorado

Kansas City

Las Vegas

Grand Canyon

Mount Elbert

U N I T E D

Los Angeles

American Indians

O F   A M

farming

sea lions

San Diego

Phoenix

surfing

oil field

Dallas

muffins

②

Pacific Ocean

Rio Grande

Houston

oil refine

oil platf

The United States of America is a huge country. It is made up of 50 states (including Alaska and Hawaii). The first people to live here were the American Indians. Today people from all over the world live in the USA. Many big cities are found in the northeast.

①

6

Ⓐ

Ⓑ

Ⓒ

M E X I C O

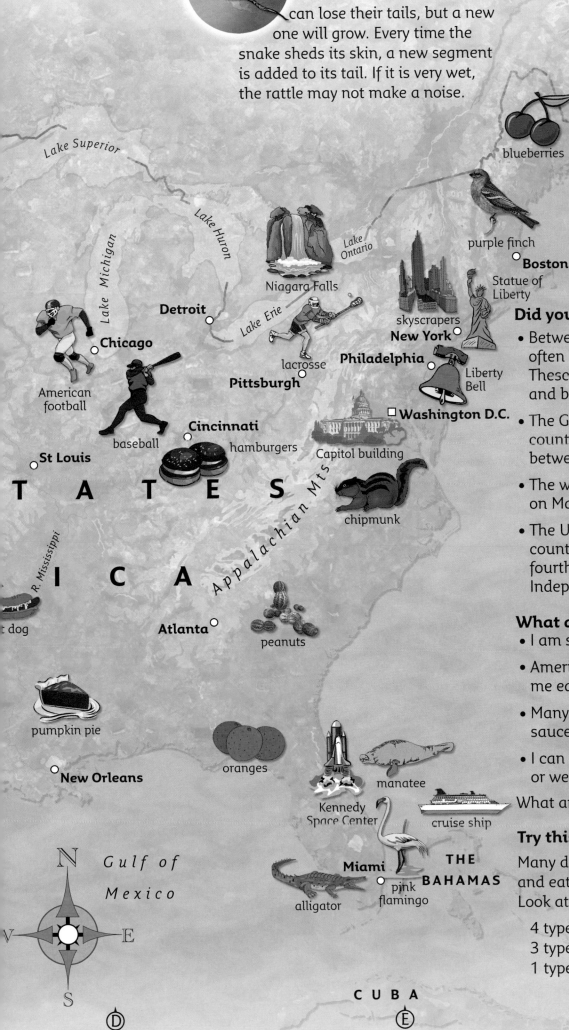

It's a fact

A rattle snake is poisonous. Its tail makes a noise like a rattle. Sometimes rattle snakes can lose their tails, but a new one will grow. Every time the snake sheds its skin, a new segment is added to its tail. If it is very wet, the rattle may not make a noise.

blueberries

Lake Superior

Lake Huron

Lake Michigan

Lake Ontario

Lake Erie

Niagara Falls

purple finch

Atlantic Ocean

Boston

Statue of Liberty

skyscrapers

New York

Detroit

Chicago

lacrosse

Philadelphia

Liberty Bell

American football

baseball

Pittsburgh

Cincinnati

hamburgers

□ **Washington D.C.**

Capitol building

St Louis

chipmunk

T A T E S

I C A

Appalachian Mts

R. Mississippi

t dog

Atlanta

peanuts

pumpkin pie

oranges

New Orleans

Kennedy Space Center

manatee

cruise ship

Miami

pink flamingo

THE BAHAMAS

alligator

N
W E
S

Gulf of Mexico

C U B A

Ⓓ   Ⓔ

Did you know?

- Between July and November there are often hurricanes in the south USA. These strong winds can destroy crops and buildings.
- The Great Lakes in the north of the country form some of the border between the USA and Canada.
- The world's first skyscrapers were built on Manhattan Island, in New York.
- The USA became an independent country on 4 July 1776. Today the fourth of July is a holiday called Independence Day.

What am I?

- I am something to eat.
- Americans eat about 7 billion of me each year.
- Many people eat me with tomato sauce or mustard.
- I can be called a frankfurter, wiener or weenie.

What am I?

Try this?

Many different types of food are grown and eaten in the USA.
Look at the map and find

4 types of fruit
3 types of snack
1 type of nut

Answers at the back of the atlas.

Mexico and the Caribbean

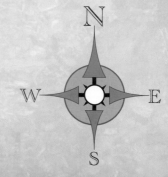

N
W   E
S

Ciudad Juárez

UNITED STATES

OF AMERICA

Baja California

Gulf of California

Rio Grande

cactus

S i e r r a

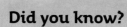
Gila monster

④

great white shark

elephant seal

donkey

Torreón

M
a
d
r
e

Gulf of

Mexico

Tabasco sauce

Monterrey

tortilla

M E X I C O

tacos

León

Guadalajara

football

Mexico City

Toluca

Mexican hat

Puebla

Mexican pyramid

Mexican temple

bul
fighti

Yucatán

BELI

Belmopan

GUATEMALA

coro

Guatemala City

H O N

Teguci

San Salvador

EL SALVADOR

Did you know?

- The country name Panama means 'place of many fish'.

③

- It took over 30 years to build the Panama canal.

- Around 35 species of lobster live in the Caribbean Sea.

- In Tobago, goat racing is one of the most popular sports.

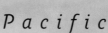
sun bathing

red chilli

What am I?

- I like to live in hot, dry places.

- I can live without rain for a long time.

②
- I do not have leaves and I am often spiny.

- I can hold lots of water.

- Sometimes I am grown as a houseplant.

What am I?

turtle

Try this!

Many different species of fish and birds are found in this region.
Look at the map and find

P a c i f i c

6 types of fish and sea animals

O c e a n

①
2 types of bird

Answers at the back of the atlas.

Ⓐ   Ⓑ   Ⓒ

The land between the USA and South America is known as Central America. Mexico is the largest country here. There is dry desert in northern Mexico and wet rainforest in southern Central America. The Caribbean is the area to the east, where there are hundreds of tropical islands.

Bermuda

A t l a n t i c
O c e a n

cruise ship

□ **Nassau**   **T H E**
               B A H A M A S

Havana □

C U B A   Monarch butterfly

cigars

sugar cane

mangoes   reggae singer

Turks and Caicos Islands

limes

Cayman Is

butterflies

JAMAICA □ **Kingston**

Rum

rum

gourds

HAITI
Port-au-
Prince □

DOMINICAN
REPUBLIC
Santo Domingo □

bananas

parrot

San Juan □

PUERTO RICO

radio telescope

cruise ship **ST KITTS AND NEVIS**
Anguilla

ANTIGUA AND BARBUDA

Montserrat
Guadeloupe

volcano

DOMINICA
Martinique
ST LUCIA   pineapples

ST VINCENT AND
THE GRENADINES   **BARBADOS**

GRENADA

sea horse

yachting **TRINIDAD & TOBAGO**

cricket

C a r i b b e a n   *S e a*

ba ... ng

butterflies

bananas

RAGUA
agua

Lake Nicaragua toucan

tropical fish

monk seal

oil platform

Aruba

V E N E Z U E L A

TA RICA
□ **San José**

Panama Canal

Panama City
P A N A M A □ coconuts

coffee

monkey

C O L O M B I A

It's a fact

Sea horses are a species of fish. They live in warm tropical waters. They eat slowly, sucking up food through their long noses. Sea horses can move their eyes all around, without moving their bodies. They wrap their long, curly tails around seaweed to stay in one place.

Ⓓ   Ⓔ   Ⓕ   9

South America

⑦ South America stretches farther south from the equator than all the other continents. The longest mountain range in the world, the Andes, runs the full length of the continent. The Amazon rainforest is the largest in the world. Colourful birds and butterflies, giant snakes, jaguars, monkeys and pumas can all be found in this lush forest. People speak

⑥ Portuguese in Brazil, but Spanish in other countries.

N
W   E
S

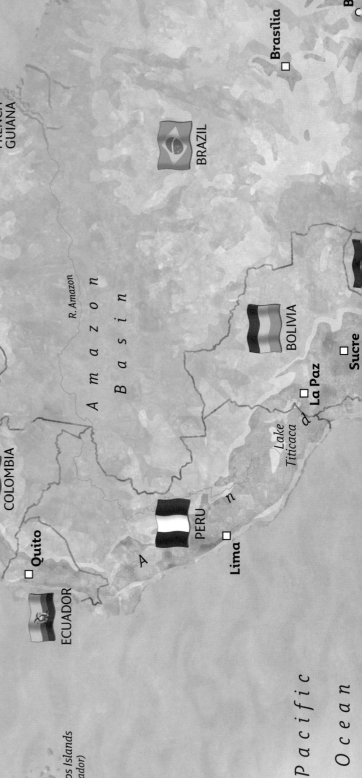

Atlantic Ocean

Cayenne
Paramaribo
Georgetown
□
FRENCH GUIANA
SURINAME
□
GUYANA
□

TRINIDAD & TOBAGO
Port of Spain
□

Caracas
□
VENEZUELA

BRAZIL

Bogotá
□
COLOMBIA

Quito
□
ECUADOR

R. Amazon

A m a z o n   B a s i n

Brasília
□

Belo Horizonte
○

BOLIVIA

Sucre
□

La Paz
□

Lake Titicaca

Lima
□
PERU

A

⑤

Pacific Ocean

Galapagos Islands (Ecuador)

CHILE

Aconcagua ▲

S

Santiago □

Buenos Aires □

ARGENTINA

Montevideo □
URUGUAY

Asunción ■

Tierra del Fuego

Falkland Islands (UK)

South Georgia (UK)

People facts

- Population: 375 000 000
- Country with most people: Brazil 186 405 00C
- City with most people: São Paulo 18 333 000

Geography facts

- Area: 17 815 420 square kilometres (6 878 572 square miles)
- Largest country: Brazil 8 514 879 square kilometres (3 287 613 square miles)
- Longest river: Amazon 6516 kilometres (4049 miles)
- Highest mountain: Aconcagua 6959 metres (22 834 feet)
- Largest lake: Lake Titicaca 8340 square kilometres (3220 square miles)
- Largest island: Tierra del Fuego 47 000 square kilometres (18 147 square miles)

Try this!

Find 2 countries beginning with the letter C.

Find 2 capital cities beginning with the letter B.

Answers at the back of the atlas.

Did you know?

- La Paz is the world's highest capital city.
- Columbia was named after Christopher Columbus.
- More than 2000 different species of butterflies are found in the rainforests of South America.
- Alpacas live in the mountains of Peru, Bolivia and Chile. They come in over 22 colours and do not like being touched.
- Ecuador is the world's leading exporter of bananas.

S o u t h e r n   O c e a n

A N T A R C T I C A

A ③ ② ① B C D

South America North

Most people in this area live on the low land near the coast.
Ecuador is the Spanish word for equator. The equator is an
imaginary line around the middle of the earth. Many unique
species of animal live in the area. Potatoes, peppers and
beans have been grown here for thousands of years.

*Caribbean
Sea*

④

Barranquilla
Cartagena

Maracaibo

Caracas

Port of Sp
TRINID
& TOBA

Barquisimeto   Valencia

oil refineries

oil
wells

PANAMA

R. Orinoco

iguana

VENEZUELA

GUY

Bucaramanga

jaguar

puma

Angel
Falls

poi
arr
fr

Medellín

G u i a n a

coffee

Bogotá

③

emeralds

Cali

COLOMBIA

R. Negro

Quito

Mount
Cotopaxi

ECUADOR

coffee

butterflies

Ma

manta ray

tapir

football

Guayaquil

A m a z o n

②

capybara

B a s i n

condor

R. Madeira

anaconda

panpipes

B

monkeys

*Pacific
Ocean*

llama

A n d e s

deforestation

①

PERU

rubber

12   Ⓐ

Lima

coffee

Ⓑ

BOLIVIA

Ⓒ

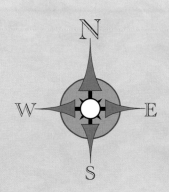

It's a fact

Andean panpipes are musical instruments made from pipes strapped together. The pipes are made from a reed called 'songo'. Songo grows on the banks of Lake Titicaca. Andean panpipes are also called zampoñas.

Did you know?

- The River Amazon carries more water than the rivers Nile, Chang Jiang and Mississippi combined.

- The Amazon is the largest rainforest in the world. About half of the world's plants, animals and insects are found there.

- The world's highest railway station, La Galera, is in Peru.

What am I?

- I live in the mountains and can reach more than 50 years of age.

- I can glide through the air for very long distances.

- Sometimes I eat so much that I can't get off the ground to fly.

- I am one of the world's largest vultures.

What am I?

Try this!

Look at the map and find

2 precious stones
1 deadly snake

Answers at the back of the atlas.

getown

Paramaribo
□

rocket
launch

Cayenne
□

FRENCH
GUIANA

URINAME

l a n d s

cayenne
peppers

*Atlantic
Ocean*

R. Amazon

Belém

Fortaleza

toucan

armadillo

sugar cane

Natal

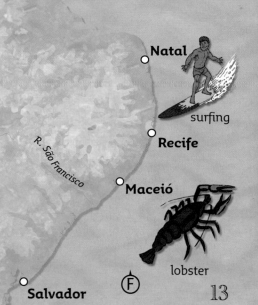

surfing

R   A   Z   I   L

R. São Francisco

Recife

porcupines

R. Tocantins

*Brazilian
Highlands*

Maceió

rot

Ⓓ diamonds

Ⓔ

Ⓕ

lobster

Salvador

13

South America South

⑦ Running down the west coast of this area is the driest place on earth, the Atacama Desert. The southern tip of South America is very cold and there are icebergs in the sea. Many people in Paraguay are descended from the Indians who lived in South America before people from Europe arrived.

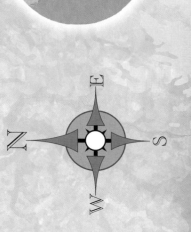

N
E
S
W

Brazilian

Planalto do Mato Grosso

B R A Z I L

B

coffee growing

Highlands

Statue de Jesus

○ **Belo Horizonte**

beaches

○ **Rio de Janeiro**

carnivals

Campinas ○

○ **São Paulo**

Santos ○

oranges

○ **Curitiba**

○ **Brasília** □

○ **Goiânia**

footballer

R. Paraná

Iguaçu Falls

football

PARAGUAY

□ **Asunción**

R. Paraguay

Gran Chaco

Gran

sheep

R. Paraná

Argentinian church

R. Salado

A

PERU

Lake Titicaca

skiing

□ **La Paz**

alpaca

potatoes

B O L I V I A

○ **Santa Cruz**

Sucre □

man in poncho

anteater

Atacama Desert

S

Chilean stag beetle

E

chinchilla

e

p

pelican

N

Did you know?
• Chile is 10 times longer than it is wide.
• The sea around Cape Horn, south of

- Millions of sheep and cattle are farmed on the flat grassy plains known as the pampas. They are looked after by Gauchos, or cowboys.
- Almost all of Paraguay's electricity comes from hydroelectric power.
- Uruguay has won several Olympic medals for football.

What am I?

- I live in the sea.
- I am black and white and have a large fin.
- I am very sociable and have a good memory.
- I am noisy. I make lots of clicks and whistles.
- I have been around for millions of years.
- I can be called Orca.

What am I?

Try this!

Look at the map and find
2 types of fish

Many sports are played in South America
Can you name 3 of these?

Answers at the back of the atlas.

It's a fact
Anteaters eat ants and termites. They have a long, sticky tongue and no teeth. Their front claws are strong and sharp. The babies ride on their mother's back.

URUGUAY

Montevideo

Rosario

Buenos Aires

Rio de la Plata

polo

wine

motor racing

tango dancers

gaucho

R. Negro

Mendoza

vineyards

Santiago

grapes

wine

Chilean chapel

puma

glaciers

fishing boats

sardines

oil tanker

Pacific Ocean

Atlantic Ocean

albatross

Falkland Islands (UK)

Tierra del Fuego

Cape Horn

penguins

elephant seals

southern whale

killer whale

South Georgia (UK)

mackerel

15

Africa

Africa is the second largest continent. It is 3 times the area of Europe. From the Mediterranean Sea in the north, Africa stretches approximately 8000 kilometres (4971 miles) to its most southerly point, Cape Agulhas. Most of northern Africa lies in and around the Sahara desert, while large areas of central Africa are covered in dense tropical rainforest.

People facts

- Population: 909 000 000
- Country with most people: Nigeria 131 530 000
- City with most people: Cairo 11 146 000

Geography facts

- Area: 30 343 578 square kilometres (11 715 721 square miles)
- Largest country: Algeria 2 381 741 square kilometres (919 595 square miles)
- Longest river: Nile 6695 kilometres (4160 miles)
- Highest mountain: Kilimanjaro 5892 metres (19 331 feet)
- Largest lake: Lake Victoria 68 800 square kilometres (26 563 square miles)
- Largest island: Madagascar 587 040 square kilometres (226 657 square miles)

EUROPE

ASIA

Mediterranean Sea

Red Sea

Atlas Mountains

S a h a r a

Azores (Portugal)

Madeira (Portugal)

Canary Is (Spain)

Rabat
MOROCCO

Laayoune
WESTERN SAHARA

Nouakchott
MAURITANIA

Dakar
SENEGAL
THE GAMBIA
Banjul
Bissau
GUINEA-BISSAU
Conakry
GUINEA
Freetown

Praia
CAPE VERDE

Algiers
ALGERIA

Tunis
TUNISIA

Tripoli
LIBYA

Cairo
EGYPT

R. Nile

Khartoum
SUDAN

Asmara
ERITREA

DJIBOUTI
Djibouti

Addis Ababa
Ethiopian Highlands

Juba
SOUTH SUDAN

CENTRAL AFRICAN REPUBLIC

Ndjamena
CHAD

NIGER

Niamey

MALI
Bamako

BURKINA
Ouagadougou

CÔTE D'IVOIRE
Yamoussoukro
GHANA
Lomé
BENIN
Porto-Novo
Abuja
NIGERIA

Monrovia

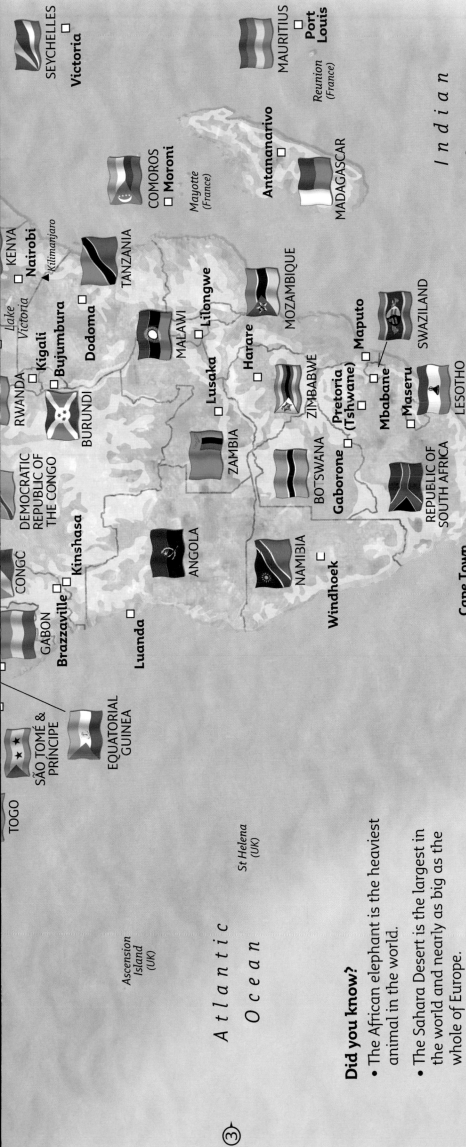

SEYCHELLES
Victoria

MAURITIUS
Port Louis

Reunion (France)

COMOROS □ **Moroni**

Mayotte (France)

Antananarivo

MADAGASCAR

I n d i a n

O c e a n

KENYA
□ **Nairobi**
▲ *Kilimanjaro*

Lake Victoria

RWANDA
□ **Kigali**
Bujumbura □

Dodoma □

TANZANIA

BURUNDI

Kinshasa □

DEMOCRATIC REPUBLIC OF THE CONGO

CONGO

Brazzaville □

GABON

Luanda □

ANGOLA

MALAWI
Lilongwe □

Lusaka □

ZAMBIA

Harare □

ZIMBABWE

MOZAMBIQUE

Maputo □

Pretoria (Tshwane) □
Mbabane □

SWAZILAND

Maseru □

LESOTHO

Gaborone □

BOTSWANA

REPUBLIC OF SOUTH AFRICA

Cape Agulhas

Windhoek □

NAMIBIA

Cape Town □

TOGO

SÃO TOMÉ & PRÍNCIPE

EQUATORIAL GUINEA

St Helena (UK)

Ascension Island (UK)

A t l a n t i c

O c e a n

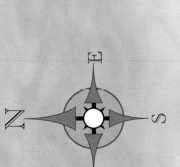

Did you know?

- The African elephant is the heaviest animal in the world.

- The Sahara Desert is the largest in the world and nearly as big as the whole of Europe.

- Mount Kenya is on the equator, but its peak is always covered in snow.

- About 400 languages are spoken in Nigeria.

- The Goliath beetle found near the equator in Africa is one of the largest insects in the world.

- In the rainforests of central Africa, it rains almost every day.

- The sea around the Cape of Good Hope is rough and dangerous. Gale force winds blow there most of the time.

Try this!

Unscramble these letters to find the country.
Clue: It is surrounded by sea.

CARDAMSAGA

Answers at the back of the atlas.

N
W — E
S

Ⓐ   Ⓑ   Ⓒ

① ② ③

17

Northern Africa

⑤

Did you know?

- There are over 500 tribes in Sudan. The tribes speak more than 100 different languages.

- Although there are many different languages, most people in northern Africa can speak Arabic.

- In Nigeria, twins are always called the same names. The first twin is called Taiwo. The second twin is called Kehinde.

④

- In Egypt, many people live on the banks of the River Nile, where they can grow food.

- Lake Chad is very shallow and is shrinking fast.

What am I?

②

- I am used for transport, milk, meat and wool.

- I can survive without water for about 2 weeks and without food for around a month.

- My thick coat reflects sunshine and my long eyelashes protect my eyes from sand.

- I can have one or two humps.

What am I?

Answers at the back of the atlas.

①

PORTUGAL
SPAIN

Mediter

Algiers

spices

citrus fruit

grapes

Madeira
(Portugal)

Rabat
Casablanca

MOROCCO

Atlas Mts

Berber architecture

Canary Is
(Spain)

carpets

oasis

Laayoune

WESTERN SAHARA

ALGERIA

S *a*

date palm

cactus

dates

sand

MAURITANIA

baboon

camel

CAPE VERDE

Nouakchott

R. Sénégal

MALI

R. Niger

N

Praia

③

Dakar

SENEGAL

Banjul
THE GAMBIA

S *a* *h* *e* *l*

groundnuts

Niamey

beach resort

Bissau

pygmy hippopotamus

Bamako

BURKINA

GUINEA-BISSAU

GUINEA

hoopoe

Ouagadougou

Conakry

Freetown

GHANA

BENIN

TOGO

NIG

SIERRA LEONE

CÔTE D'IVOIRE

bananas

cocoa

Lake Volta

Lomé

Ab

Monrovia

Yamoussoukro

football

Lagos

LIBERIA

Accra

Porto-Novo

coconuts

Gulf of Guinea

Mt Cam
Malabo

EQU
GU

oil

São Tom

SÃO TOMÉ AND PRÍNCIPE

Libr

Atlantic Ocean

N

W   E

S

18   Ⓐ   Ⓑ   Ⓒ

Africa is connected to the continent of Asia at the narrow Sinai peninsula, north of the Red Sea. It is separated narrowly from Europe by the Strait of Gibraltar. Much of northern Africa is dry desert: the Sahara Desert and the Sahel region.

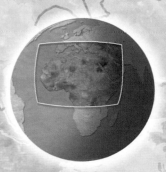

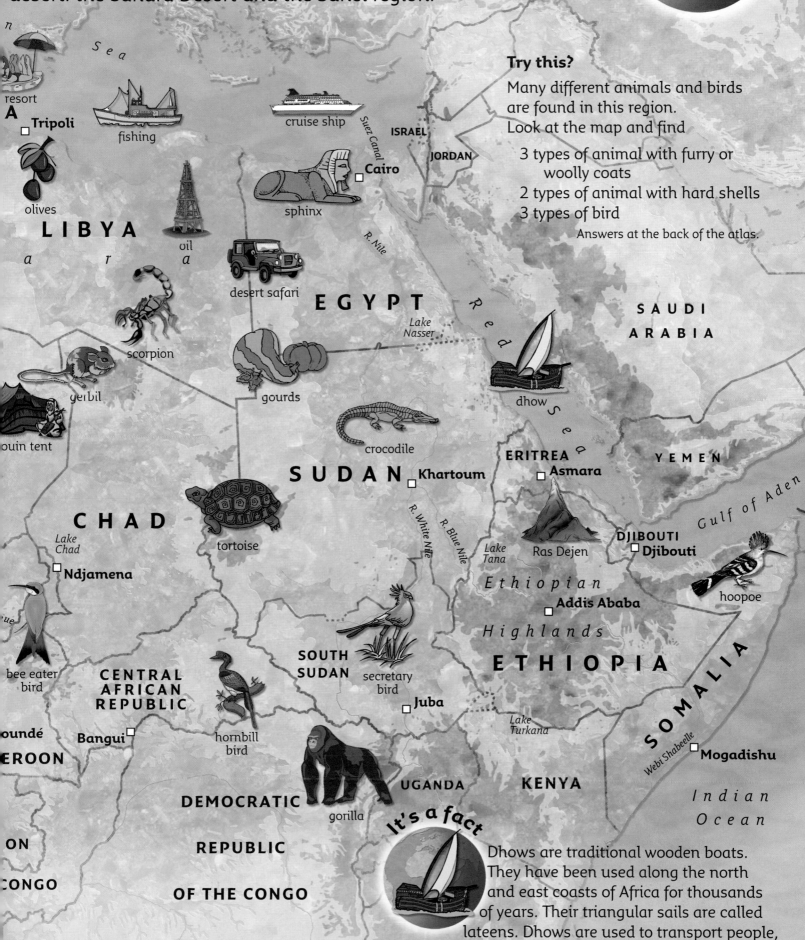

Sea

resort

A

Tripoli

fishing

olives

cruise ship

ISRAEL

JORDAN

Suez Canal

sphinx

Cairo

R. Nile

L I B Y A

oil

a   *r*   *a*

desert safari

E G Y P T

Lake Nasser

Red

S A U D I ARABIA

scorpion

gerbil

ouin tent

gourds

dhow

Sea

Try this?

Many different animals and birds are found in this region.
Look at the map and find

3 types of animal with furry or woolly coats
2 types of animal with hard shells
3 types of bird

Answers at the back of the atlas.

crocodile

ERITREA

Asmara

Y E M E N

S U D A N   **Khartoum**

Gulf of Aden

CHAD

Lake Chad

tortoise

R. White Nile

R. Blue Nile

Lake Tana

Ras Dejen

DJIBOUTI
Djibouti

hoopoe

Ndjamena

E t h i o p i a n

Addis Ababa

ue

H i g h l a n d s

bee eater bird

CENTRAL AFRICAN REPUBLIC

secretary bird

SOUTH SUDAN

E T H I O P I A

Juba

Lake Turkana

oundé

Bangui

hornbill bird

S O M A L I A

EROON

gorilla

Webi Shabeelle

Mogadishu

UGANDA

KENYA

I n d i a n

DEMOCRATIC

ON

REPUBLIC

O c e a n

ONGO

OF THE CONGO

It's a fact

Dhows are traditional wooden boats. They have been used along the north and east coasts of Africa for thousands of years. Their triangular sails are called lateens. Dhows are used to transport people, animals, fish and other goods.

ANGOLA

Ⓓ

Ⓔ   **TANZANIA**

Ⓕ

Southern Africa

⑦ At the centre of southern Africa is the huge rainforest of the River Congo and the Congo Basin. The Great Rift Valley is surrounded by some of the highest mountains in Africa. In the southwest are the Kalahari and Namib deserts.

N · E · W · S

ERITREA

DJIBOUTI

SOMALIA

Mogadishu

ETHIOPIA

Ethiopian Highlands

Lake Turkana

KENYA

coffee beans

elephants

lion

beaches

Dar es Salaam

cloves

Moroni

COMOROS

Indian Ocean

SUDAN

Nairobi

Lake Victoria

UGANDA

Kampala

Juba

secretary bird

SOUTH SUDAN

gorilla

Kilimanjaro

Dodoma

leopard

Great Rift Valley

TANZANIA

Lake Nyasa

MAL

RWANDA

Kigali

Bujumbura

BURUNDI

Lake Tanganyika

cheetah

Lubumbashi

CENTRAL AFRICAN REPUBLIC

Bangui

hombill bird

R. Congo

DEMOCRATIC

REPUBLIC

OF

Congo Basin

crocodiles

deforestation

THE

CONGO

elephants

NIGERIA

CAMEROON

Yaoundé

chimpanzee

Brazzaville

Kinshasa

ANGOLA

C O N G O

GABON

Libreville

Malabo

EQUATORIAL GUINEA

São Tomé

SÃO TOMÉ AND PRÍNCIPE

flying fish

ANGOLA

Luanda

oil rig

Bié

⑥

⑤

MADAGASCAR

Antananarivo

crocodiles

lemur

Mozambique Channel

aardvark

port

MOZAMBIQUE

ZIMBABWE
Harare

rhinoceros

R. Limpopo

Victoria Falls

Maputo

Mbabane
SWAZILAND

Zulu warrior

Zulu house

Durban

BOTSWANA

Kalahari Desert

meerkat

Gaborone

Pretoria

Johannesburg

Maseru
LESOTHO

Drakensberg

REPUBLIC OF SOUTH AFRICA

gold mines

R. Orange

oryx

oranges

Port Elizabeth

cricket

NAMIBIA

rhinoceros

Windhoek

rugby

sand dunes

Namib Desert

grapes

Cape Town
Cape of Good Hope

ostrich

penguins

sharks

A t l a n t i c   O c e a n

sardines

What am I?

- I am found on the coast and in deserts.
- I can be made from worn down stone and shell.
- I move in the wind and get very hot in the sun.
- I can be different shapes: ridges, crescents and crests like waves.
- I can fall downhill in an avalanche, like snow.
- I am made from sand.

What am I?

Try this?

There are lots of different fruits and plants in this region.
Look at the map and find

2 types of fruit
1 type of spice.

Answers at the back of the atlas.

Did you know?

- Madagascar is the only place in the world where lemurs live.
- A lemur is a type of monkey with a long tail.
- Nelson Mandela became the first black president of South Africa in 1994.
- European languages such as French, Portuguese and English are widely spoken in southern Africa.
- Diamonds and gold are mined in southern Africa.

It's a fact

Gorillas are the largest type of ape in the world.
They live on the ground in the forests of Africa. Gorillas are a close relative to humans. They eat fruits, leaves and insects. Gorillas are in danger of becoming extinct.

Ⓐ Ⓑ Ⓒ Ⓓ

① ② ③

21

Europe

The land area of Europe covers just over 2% of the world. It is the second smallest continent and extends far north into the Arctic Ocean and south to the Mediterranean Sea. In the north the winters are long and cold. In the south the weather is much warmer. Europe has over 40 countries and a wide variety of cultures, languages and religions.

④

People facts
- Population: 586 000 000 (excluding Russian Federation)
- Country with most people: Germany 82 689 000
- City with most people: Paris 9 854 000

Geography facts
③
- Area: 9 908 599 square kilometres (3 825 731 square miles)
- Largest country: Ukraine 603 700 square kilometres (233 090 square miles) (excluding Russian Federation)
- Longest river: Volga 3688 kilometres (2291 miles)
- Highest mountain: El'brus 5642 metres (18 510 feet)
②
- Largest lake: Caspian Sea 371 000 square kilometres (143 243 square miles)
- Largest island: Great Britain 218 476 square kilometres (84 354 square miles)

Try this!
How many flags are black, red and yellow?

Which flag has 5 blue stripes?

Which country uses this flag?

①

Answers at the back of the atlas.

ICELAND
□ Reykjavík

Faroe Islands (Denmark)

UNITED KINGDOM

Dublin □

Great Britain

NETHERL
Amster
The Hague
Bru □

IRELAND

London □

BELGIUM

Paris □

LUXEMB

Atlantic Ocean

FRANCE

SWITZE

ANDORRA

MONA

PORTUGAL

Madrid □

Barcelona

Lisbon □

SPAIN

Gibraltar (UK)

A F R I C

Ⓐ   Ⓑ   Ⓒ

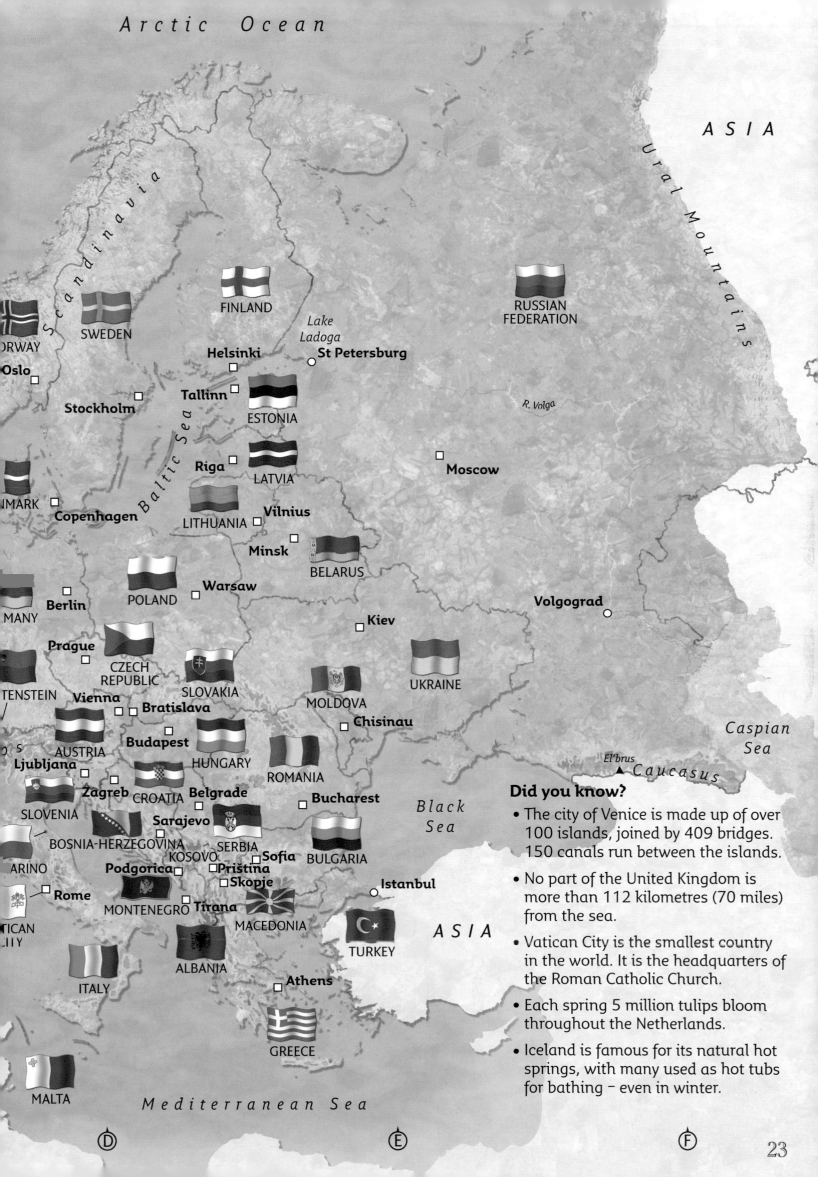

Arctic Ocean

ASIA

Ural Mountains

NORWAY
Oslo

SWEDEN

FINLAND

Lake Ladoga

RUSSIAN FEDERATION

R. Volga

Helsinki

St Petersburg

Stockholm

Tallinn

ESTONIA

Moscow

DENMARK

Riga

LATVIA

Copenhagen

Vilnius

LITHUANIA

Volgograd

Minsk

BELARUS

Baltic Sea

Berlin

POLAND

Warsaw

GERMANY

Kiev

Prague

CZECH REPUBLIC

SLOVAKIA

UKRAINE

LIECHTENSTEIN

Vienna

Bratislava

MOLDOVA

Caspian Sea

AUSTRIA

Budapest

Chisinau

Ljubljana

HUNGARY

El'brus ▲ *Caucasus*

Zagreb

CROATIA

Belgrade

ROMANIA

SLOVENIA

Sarajevo

Bucharest

Black Sea

SAN MARINO

BOSNIA-HERZEGOVINA

KOSOVO

SERBIA

Sofia

Did you know?

Rome

Podgorica

Priština

BULGARIA

- The city of Venice is made up of over 100 islands, joined by 409 bridges. 150 canals run between the islands.

VATICAN CITY

Skopje

Istanbul

MONTENEGRO

Tirana

MACEDONIA

ASIA

- No part of the United Kingdom is more than 112 kilometres (70 miles) from the sea.

ITALY

ALBANIA

TURKEY

- Vatican City is the smallest country in the world. It is the headquarters of the Roman Catholic Church.

Athens

- Each spring 5 million tulips bloom throughout the Netherlands.

GREECE

- Iceland is famous for its natural hot springs, with many used as hot tubs for bathing – even in winter.

MALTA

Mediterranean Sea

Ⓓ   Ⓔ   Ⓕ

23

United Kingdom and Ireland

⑦

The United Kingdom is made up of 4 nations: England, Wales, Scotland and Northern Ireland. Its capital and largest city is London. Great Britain is the largest island in Europe and is separated from mainland Europe by only 35 kilometres (21 miles) at the Strait of Dover. Ireland, whose capital is Dublin, is a separate country from Northern Ireland.

⑥

Did you know?

- More than 6000 islands make up the United Kingdom and Ireland.
- Some areas of Ireland have more wet days than dry days.
- The city of Edinburgh is built on an extinct volcano.
- More than 300 different languages are spoken in London.
- The Welsh language is spoken and written in Wales.
- Many tourists come to these islands to visit the castles, churches and ancient buildings.
- Football, rugby and cricket are popular sports.

What am I?

- I am green. Mostly I have white flowers.
- I usually have 3 leaves.
- Ancient people thought I was magical.
- I am strongly associated with Ireland.

What am I?

Answers at the back of the atlas.

Try this!

Many different sports are popular in the United Kingdom. Look at the map and find

3 sports played with a ball
1 sport that takes place on water
2 sports that need ice or snow

Answers at the back of the atlas.

⑤

Shetland Islands

Orkney Islands

Atlantic

Ocean

Lewis

Outer Hebrides

The Minch

Skye

Inner Hebrides

golden eagle

Highland cattle

Moray Firth

Inverness

Loch Ness

Ben Nevis

Fort William

Grampian Mts

SCOTLAND

Jura

curling

skiing

oil rig

Aberdeen

fishing boat

Highland piper

Dundee

Edinburgh

Firth of Forth

It's a fact

Red buses have been used in London since the 1950s. They replaced trams and trolley buses. They can be single or double decked. Open-topped buses are popular with tourists. The London bus network is one of the largest in the world. Every weekday 6 million passengers are carried over 700 different routes.

25

Northern Europe

□ **Reykjavík**
ICELAND

glaciers

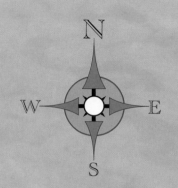

Northern Europe has a rugged landscape and many of its countries are almost completely surrounded by sea. In the far north winters can be extremely cold and the seas may freeze for several months. Most people live in the south of this region where the climate is milder.

Faroe Is
(Denmark)

Did you know?

- The Baltic Sea borders on 9 countries. Parts of it can be frozen for 6 months of the year.
- Brittany is a region in northwest France. The people there speak Breton.
- Puppets are popular in the Czech Republic. They are used to entertain people and tell stories.
- German is spoken in Austria, Switzerland and Germany.

What am I?

- I have large round eyes, a sharp beak and claws.
- I fly about at night and I sleep during the day.
- I hunt small animals, insects and fish.
- I build nests in trees, barns and sometimes underground.

What am I?

Try this!

Many different types of food are grown or manufactured in this region. Look at the map and find

   1 type of cheese
   3 types of farm animal
   1 type of pastry

Answers at the back of the atlas.

salmon

fishing boats

Highland piper

oil rigs

Norwe...
chu...

DE

N o r t h

S e a

pi...

shamrock

Edinburgh Castle

IRELAND

□ **Dublin**

harp

sheep

UNITED

windmills

KINGDOM

NETHERLANDS

Tower Bridge

Amsterdam
The Hague □

Gouda cheese

rugby

London

□ **Brussels**

BELGIUM

G

□ **R. Rhine**

Frankf...

A t l a n t i c
O c e a n

English Channel

LUXEMBOURG

Luxembourg □

Mont St Michel

R. Loire

Paris

R. Seine

owl

seafood

Arc de Triomphe

Eiffel Tower

Bern □

SWITZERLAN...

Bay of
Biscay

F R A N C E

croissants

Massif
Central

I T...

Arctic Ocean

blue whale

puffin

owl

reindeer

ning

moose

eider duck

Kola Peninsula

fishing through ice

White Sea

wheat farming

R. Northern Dvina

wild mushrooms

paper making

lynx

R U S S I A N

skiing

saunas

Lake Ladoga

Lake Onega

beavers

R. Sukhona

wild horses

Oslo

Vänern

Stockholm

Helsinki

FINLAND

Tallinn

St Petersburg

Winter Palace

ESTONIA

F E D E R A T I O N

Vättern

LATVIA

dairy cows

Moscow

Kremlin

Volga Uplands

badger

Riga

R. Dvina

Plain

enhagen

LITHUANIA

Vilnius

potatoes

R. Dnieper

Central Russian

Baltic Sea

RUS. FED.

Minsk

Russian dolls

Uplands

wind farms

he

Berlin

North European

BELARUS

boar

R. Vistula

Warsaw

POLAND

brown bears

UKRAINE

R. Dniester

It's a fact

glass making

Prague

CZECH REPUBLIC

ball

castle

SLOVAKIA

Bratislava

Carpathian Mts

Vienna

R. Danube

Budapest

MOLDOVA

Chisinau

AUSTRIA

HUNGARY

castle

ROMANIA

NY

NORWAY

SWEDEN

Glass is made from sand. The sand is heated to a high temperature until it melts. Many items we use every day are made from glass. It is transparent – we can see through it. Sometimes metals are added to glass to change its colour. Brightly coloured stained glass is often found in church windows.

D   E   F

27

Southern Europe

DENMARK

North Sea

⑤

Hamburg

N
W **E**
S

UNITED KINGDOM

NETHERLANDS
Amsterdam
The Hague
London

Hannover

Berl

R. Rhine

G E R M A N

English Channel

Brussels

Cologne

BELGIUM

Frankfurt

LUXEMBOURG

Atlantic Ocean

④

R. Seine

Paris

Eiffel Tower

Arc de Triomphe

apples
R. Loire

F R A N C E

croissants

Swiss cheese

grapes

football

Munich

seafood

Bay of Biscay

wine

cheese

Massif Central

Bern
LIECHTENSTEIN
SWITZERLAND

Mont Blanc

cathedral

Milan

A

gondol

swordfish

Cantabrian Mts

garlic

R. Rhône

skiing

R. Po

skiing

Oporto

P
O
R
T
U
G
A
L

Spanish guitar

bull fighting

skiing

ANDORRA

Pyrenees

Marseille

MONACO

cars

casinos

Apennines

③

R. Tagus

Madrid

S P A I N

Barcelona

port

Leaning Tower of Pisa

Rome

Lisbon

leather goods

beaches

cruise ships

Sardinia

Colosseum

sardines

oranges

flamenco dancers

almonds

Balearic Islands

grapes

Tyrrhenian Sea

Strait of Gibraltar

M

e

d

i

t

e

Si

②

MOROCCO

ALGERIA

TUNISIA

The south of this region lies on the shores of the warm Mediterranean Sea where many people spend their holidays. Southern Europe and Africa are separated by only 15 kilometres (9 miles) of water known as the Strait of Gibraltar, which links the Atlantic Ocean and the Mediterranean Sea. Two of the world's smallest countries, Vatican City and Monaco, are in Southern Europe.

①

A F

Ⓐ

Ⓑ

Ⓒ

Warsaw

POLAND

cathedral

que

ECH
UBLIC

glass making

SLOVAKIA

na

Bratislava

HUNGARY

Budapest

Hungarian church

NIA

ljana

Zagreb

ATIA

Croatian house

Belgrade

BOSNIA-
HERZEGOVINA

Sarajevo

SERBIA

MONTENEGRO

Priština

Sofia

Podgorica

KOSOVO

Skopje

ALBANIA

MACEDONIA

atic Sea

pizza

Tirana

s

etti

olives

Greek church

Greek pottery

GREECE

Athens

Parthenon

Ionian Sea

cano

etta

A

fishing boats

Cretan mosque

Crete

Knossos

Carpathian Mts

brown bears

R. Dniester

MOLDOVA

Chisinau

castle

ROMANIA

Bucharest

roses

R. Danube

Balkan Mts

BULGARIA

grapes

Black Sea

Istanbul

fortress

TURKEY

Izmir

Aegean Sea

kebabs

n

e

a

n

S

e

a

LIBYA

EGYPT

UKRAINE

Kiev

Did you know?

- The islands of Sicily and Sardinia belong to Italy.

- Venice is built on a large area of water, called a lagoon.

- In Albania and Bulgaria nodding your head means no. Shaking your head from side to side means yes.

- In France April Fool's Day is known as April Fish Day.

- Portugal has the world's largest solar powered electricity plant.

- The wristwatch was invented in Switzerland.

- The River Danube flows through 7 countries.

What am I?

- I am made from flour, and egg or water.
- I am cooked quickly in boiling water.
- I am often covered in tomato sauce.
- My name means 'thin string'.
- I am a type of pasta.

What am I?

Answers at the back of the atlas.

Try this!

Many famous buidings and ruins are found in this region.
Look at the map and find

Arc de Triomphe
Colosseum
Knossos
Parthenon
Leaning Tower of Pisa

D   E   F

Asia

Asia is the largest continent. It is bigger than Europe and Africa combined. Asia extends from the Ural mountains to the Pacific Ocean in the east and from the Arctic Ocean to the Indian Ocean in the south. Climates vary from the cold Arctic in the north to hot tropical in the south.

Arcti

N
W   E
S

EUROPE

Moscow

RUSSIA
FEDERAT

S   i

Ural Mountains

④

CYPRUS

LEBANON

ISRAEL

Black
Sea

Ankara

TURKEY

GEORGIA

T'bilisi

Yerevan

AZERBAIJAN

Baku

SYRIA

Damascus

ARMENIA

Caspian
Sea

UZBEKISTAN

Astana

KAZAKHSTAN

Bishkek

Tashkent

KYRGYZSTAN

③

JORDAN

Amman

Baghdad

Tehran

IRAQ

Kuwait

KUWAIT

IRAN

Ashgabat

TURKMENISTAN

Dushanbe

TAJIKISTAN

Kabul

Islamabad

AFGHANISTAN

Kunlun Shan

Plateau
of Tibet

Himalaya

BAHRAIN

QATAR

SAUDI ARABIA

Riyadh

The Gulf

UNITED ARAB
EMIRATES

Muscat

PAKISTAN

New
Delhi

NEPAL

Kathmandu

Mount
Everest

BHUT

Thimp

Dhaka

②

Red Sea

AFRICA

San'a

YEMEN

OMAN

INDIA

BANGLADESH

Naypyi

MYA
(BU

Try this!

This country is also an island.
Can you name it?

Socotra
(Yemen)

Arabian
Sea

Bay of
Bengal

Yan
(Ran

Andaman Is
(India)

Nicobar Is
(India)

SRI LANKA

Sri Jayewardenepura Kotte

MALDIVES

①

Indian Ocean

Ⓐ   Ⓑ   Ⓒ

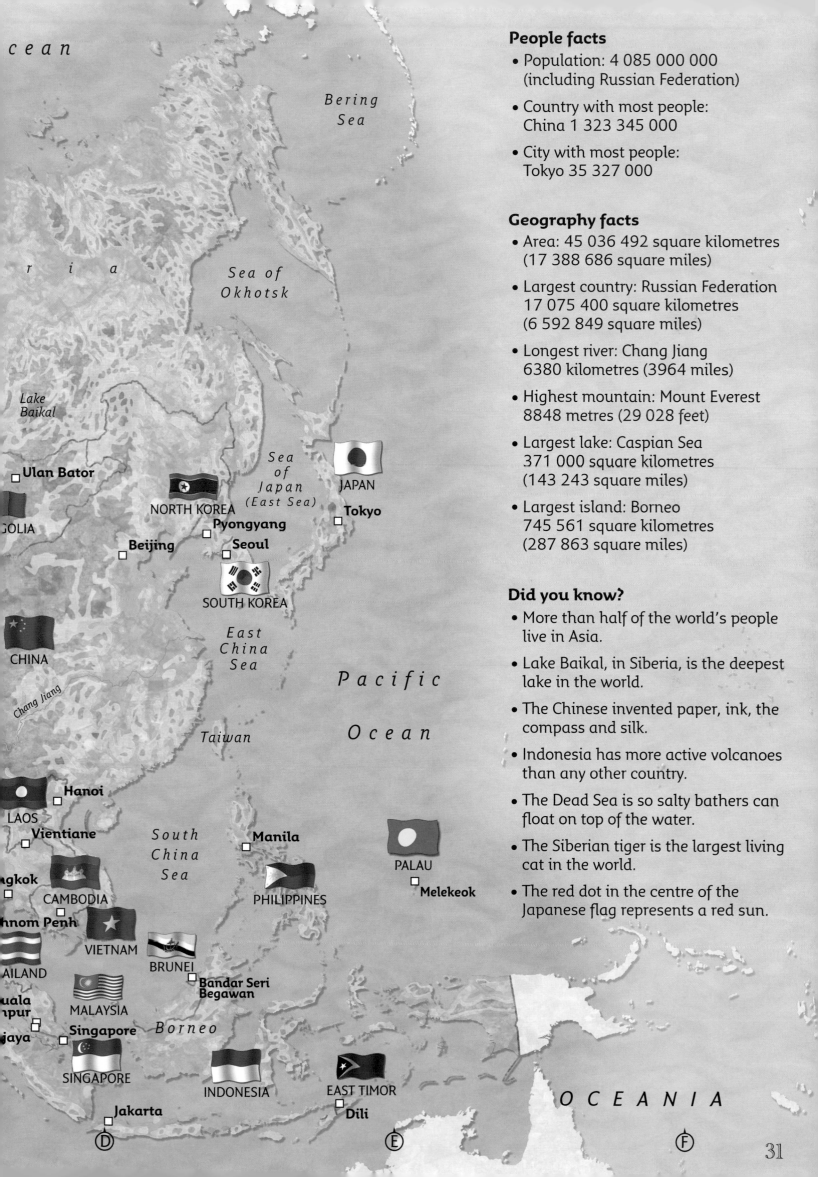

People facts

- Population: 4 085 000 000 (including Russian Federation)
- Country with most people: China 1 323 345 000
- City with most people: Tokyo 35 327 000

Geography facts

- Area: 45 036 492 square kilometres (17 388 686 square miles)
- Largest country: Russian Federation 17 075 400 square kilometres (6 592 849 square miles)
- Longest river: Chang Jiang 6380 kilometres (3964 miles)
- Highest mountain: Mount Everest 8848 metres (29 028 feet)
- Largest lake: Caspian Sea 371 000 square kilometres (143 243 square miles)
- Largest island: Borneo 745 561 square kilometres (287 863 square miles)

Did you know?

- More than half of the world's people live in Asia.
- Lake Baikal, in Siberia, is the deepest lake in the world.
- The Chinese invented paper, ink, the compass and silk.
- Indonesia has more active volcanoes than any other country.
- The Dead Sea is so salty bathers can float on top of the water.
- The Siberian tiger is the largest living cat in the world.
- The red dot in the centre of the Japanese flag represents a red sun.

c e a n

Bering Sea

Sea of Okhotsk

r i a

Lake Baikal

Ulan Bator

GOLIA

Sea of Japan (East Sea)

JAPAN

NORTH KOREA

Tokyo

Pyongyang

Beijing

Seoul

SOUTH KOREA

CHINA

East China Sea

Chang Jiang

Pacific

Taiwan

Ocean

Hanoi

LAOS

Vientiane

South China Sea

Manila

PALAU

ngkok

CAMBODIA

PHILIPPINES

Melekeok

hnom Penh

VIETNAM

BRUNEI

AILAND

Bandar Seri Begawan

uala
npur

MALAYSIA

Borneo

jaya

Singapore

SINGAPORE

INDONESIA

EAST TIMOR

Jakarta

Dili

O C E A N I A

D

E

F

31

Russian Federation

Russia is the largest country in the world. It has borders with 14 different countries. Most Russians live in the west of the country. Siberia, in the north, is almost empty. It is dry and extremely cold there. The southwest, on the coast of the Black Sea, is very warm. Much of the country is covered with huge grassy plains, known as steppes.

⑤

④

③

②

①

*Arcti
Ocea*

*Barents
Sea*

FINLAND

Baltic Sea

reindeer

fishing
in the Arctic

*Kara
Sea*

eider duck

ESTONIA

POLAND

**RUS.
FED.**

LITHUANIA

LATVIA
St Petersburg

potatoes

vodka

ice
hockey

Archangel

R. North Dvina

R. Pechora

Ural owl

Vorkuta

lynx

R. Yenisey

Si b

BELARUS

gymnastics

Kremlin

R. Dniestr

Kiev

UKRAINE

football

Moscow

**Nizhniy
Novgorod**

ballet

R U S S I

F E D E R A T

MOLDOVA

R. Dnieper

Kazan

Perm

West

Siberian

Plain

R. Ob

R. Lower Tunguska

*Sea of
Azou*

sugarbeet

R. Don

R. Volga

wheat

Yekaterinburg

Samara

Ufa

chess

cathedral

Ural Mountains

R. Yenisey

brown bea

Black Sea

balalaika

Volgograd

Chelyabinsk

Cossack
dancers

Omsk

cathedral

R. Irtysh

Novosibirsk

Krasnoyarsk

GEORGIA

ARMENIA

TURKEY

AZERBAIJAN

AZ.

Caspian
seal

Russian
dolls

K A Z A K H S T A N

Astana

Siberian stag

Caspian Sea

*Aral
Sea*

UZBEKISTAN

rocket
launch site

R. Syrdar'ya

wheat

*Lake
Balkhash*

M O N G

TURKMENISTAN

Ashgabat

R. Amudar'ya

Tashkent

Bishkek

KYRGYZSTAN

I R A N

TAJIKISTAN

AFGHANISTAN

C H

Ⓐ

Ⓑ

Ⓒ

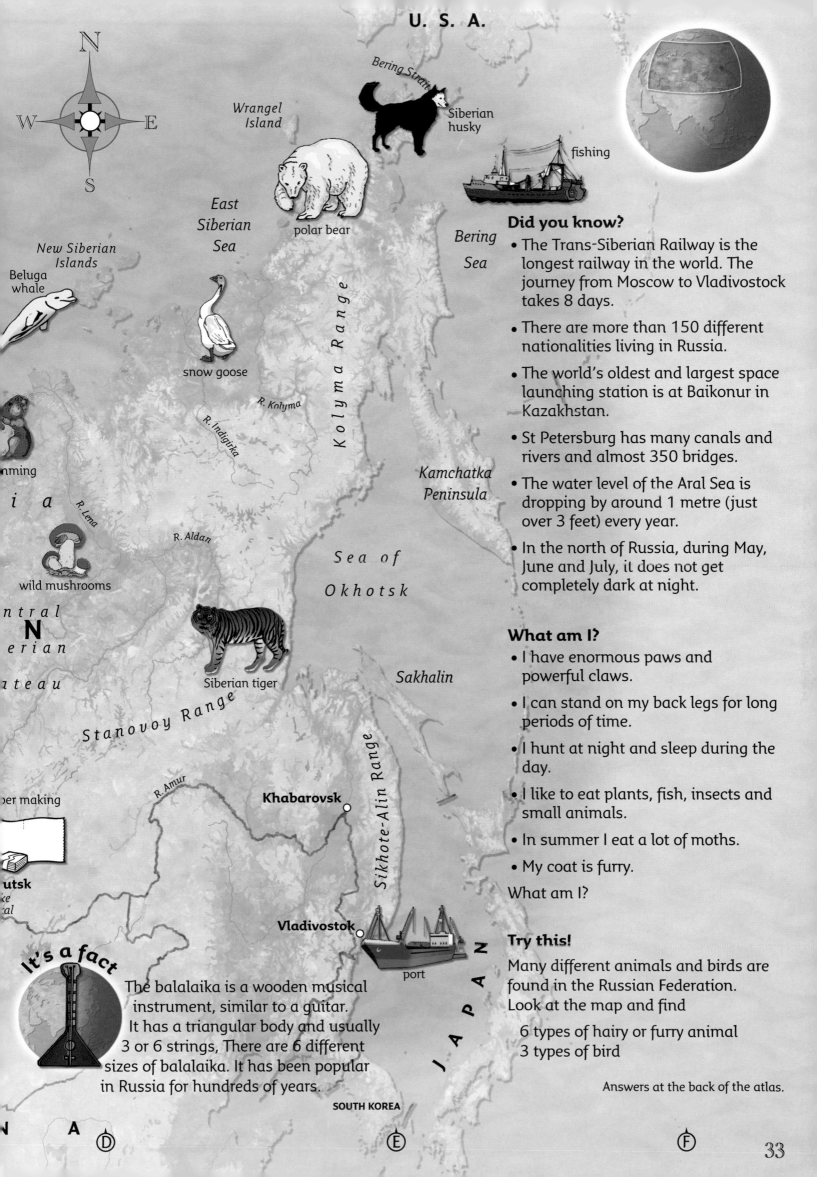

U. S. A.

Bering Strait

Wrangel Island

Siberian husky

fishing

East Siberian Sea

polar bear

New Siberian Islands

Beluga whale

snow goose

R. Kolyma

R. Indigirka

Kolyma Range

Bering Sea

...ming

R. Lena

R. Aldan

wild mushrooms

Kamchatka Peninsula

Sea of Okhotsk

...i a

...ntral
N
...erian
...teau

Siberian tiger

Sakhalin

Stanovoy Range

R. Amur

Khabarovsk

...per making

...utsk
...ke
...al

Sikhote-Alin Range

Vladivostok

port

J A P A N

SOUTH KOREA

Did you know?

- The Trans-Siberian Railway is the longest railway in the world. The journey from Moscow to Vladivostock takes 8 days.

- There are more than 150 different nationalities living in Russia.

- The world's oldest and largest space launching station is at Baikonur in Kazakhstan.

- St Petersburg has many canals and rivers and almost 350 bridges.

- The water level of the Aral Sea is dropping by around 1 metre (just over 3 feet) every year.

- In the north of Russia, during May, June and July, it does not get completely dark at night.

What am I?

- I have enormous paws and powerful claws.

- I can stand on my back legs for long periods of time.

- I hunt at night and sleep during the day.

- I like to eat plants, fish, insects and small animals.

- In summer I eat a lot of moths.

- My coat is furry.

What am I?

Try this!

Many different animals and birds are found in the Russian Federation. Look at the map and find

6 types of hairy or furry animal
3 types of bird

Answers at the back of the atlas.

It's a fact

The balalaika is a wooden musical instrument, similar to a guitar. It has a triangular body and usually 3 or 6 strings. There are 6 different sizes of balalaika. It has been popular in Russia for hundreds of years.

N ... A

Ⓓ   Ⓔ   Ⓕ   33

Southwest Asia

Black Sea

GREECE

⑤

The north and west of this area is mountainous, with high ranges extending through Turkey into Iran. The Arabian Peninsula between the Red Sea and The Gulf is mostly dry sandy desert. Water is scarce in much of Southwest Asia. Two major rivers are the Tigris and Euphrates.

④

LIBYA

Mediterranean Sea

Did you know?

- Saudi Arabia is the world's leading exporter of oil.

- Three of the world's major religions started in this area: Judaism, Christianity and Islam.

- Damascus, the capital of Syria, is one of the oldest cities in the world.

③

- The Caucasus mountain range protects Armenia, Georgia and Azerbaijan from cold north winds.

What am I?

- I am a type of bird.

- I have long, thin legs and a long neck.

- I like to wade in shallow water.

- I often stand on one leg.

②

- I eat small shrimps.

- I am pink.

What am I?

Try this!

Look at the map. Can you find these:

3 Arabian animals
1 religious building
1 sport popular in Pakistan

Answers at the back of the atlas.

①

Ⓐ

Ⓑ

Ⓒ

El'br

GEOR

kebabs

ARM

□ Ankara

mosque

coffee

Yer

Taurus Mts

TURKEY

Crusader castles

cedar trees

Nicosia □

CYPRUS

SYRIA

date palms

Beirut □

LEBANON

ISRAEL

□ Damascus

Bagh

Amman

□ □ **JORDAN**

Jerusalem

Syrian Desert

oil refineries

IRA

Cairo □

Sphinx

Dome of the Rock

Arabian fox *An Nafud*

carp

R. Nile

Bedouin tent

Arabian headdress

desert safari

scuba diving

Najd

Riy

EGYPT

Muslim praying at Mecca

SAUD

crocodile

R. Nile

Red Sea

angel fish

A s i r

SUDAN

Arabian h

dhow

San'a □

E R I T R E A

YE

Ras Dejen

ETHIOPIA

DJIBOUTI

DERATION

Caspian seal

skiing

Caspian
Sea

casus

lisi

ZERBAIJAN

Baku

carpets

oil rig

N

W   E

S

*Aral
Sea*

space
station

wheat

KAZAKHSTAN

flamingo

UZBEKISTAN

R. Sydar'ya

☐ **Tashkent**

KYRGYZSTAN

CHINA

TAJIKISTAN

R. Amudar'ya

TURKMENISTAN

jackal

☐ **Dushanbe**

Ashgabat

Elburz Mts

Tehran

onager

mosque

Hindu Kush

Karakoram Range

AFGHANISTAN

Kabul ☐

R. Indus

☐ **Islamabad**

I R A N

Zagros Mountains

Afghan hounds

Sikh

UWAIT

Kuwait

P A K I S T A N

Thar Desert

BAHRAIN

Manama ☐

QATAR

Doha

OMAN

The Gulf

Gulf of Oman

Abu Dhabi ☐

**UNITED ARAB
EMIRATES**

Muscat

cricket

R. Indus

Karachi ○

Mouths of
the Indus

I N D I A

l wells

RABIA

Arabian
camel

oryx

oil tankers

*Arabian
Sea*

b'al Khali

O M A N

date palms

octopus

It's a fact

The oryx is a type of antelope,
with long, straight horns.
The oryx became extinct in the
Arabian Peninsula in the 1970s.
It has been re-introduced but it is
being hunted for its horn. This animal
can live in the desert without water for
long periods.

date palms

Arabian
fishing boats

dates

man

great white
shark

green turtle

Ⓓ   Ⓔ   Ⓕ   35

South Asia

South Asia is a region of contrasting landscapes and weather. In the north is the great mountain range of Himalaya where the climate is harsh and few people live. The lands at the mouths of the Ganges river are low lying and flooding occurs during the heavy rains in the monsoon season. Most people live in the river valleys, plains and big cities.

What am I?

- I live in the sea, especially around coral reefs.
- I have 3 hearts and my blood is blue.
- My soft body means that I can squeeze through small spaces.

- I have a beak.
- I have 8 arms.

What am I?

Try this!

Many different animals, birds and fish are found in this region. Look at the map and find

3 members of the cat family
2 types of bird
1 type of animal with sharp spines

Answers at the back of the atlas.

C H I N A

Kunlun Shan

Plateau of Tibet

yak

Himalaya

Lhasa

Tibetan monks

Thimphu
BHUTAN

Mount Everest

Kathmandu

N E P A L

Indian rhinoceros

K2

Kashmir stag

snow leopard

Golden Temple, Amritsar

Delhi
New Delhi

Jaipur

mountain goat

Islamabad

Lahore
Faisalabad

Sikh

Thar Desert

P A K I S T A N

R. Indus

R. Brahmaputra

TAJIKISTAN

Dushanbe

Hindu Kush

Kabul

AFGHANISTAN

jackal

Afghan hound

N
W E
S

36

⑦

⑥

⑤

INDIA

MYANMAR (BURMA)

R. Irrawaddy

Chittagong — rice

Mouths of the Ganges

Kolkata — tiger

Bay of Bengal

Andaman Is (India) — seafood

Nicobar Is (India) — parakeet

Indian porcupine

peacock

Nagpur

Bhopal

Indore

Ahmadabad

Asiatic lion

cricket

Arabian Sea

Mumbai — port

Pune — hockey

R. Godavari

Western Ghats

Eastern Ghats

Deccan

Hyderabad

Vijayawada — rickshaw

Chennai

Bangalore — sitar

Trivandrum — octopus

tea — Buddhism

Sri Jayewardenepura Kotte

SRI LANKA

MALDIVES

Maldive anemonefish

coral reefs

Indian Ocean

It's a fact

The sitar is a traditional string instrument with a distinctive sound. It has been popular in India and the surrounding countries for hundreds of years. The body of a sitar is made from a gourd. The neck is made from wood. There can be between 18 and 20 strings. It is a difficult instrument to learn to play.

Did you know?

- The island of Sri Lanka is famous for growing tea.
- There are more than 25 tiger reserves in India, where the animals are protected.
- 8 of the world's 10 highest mountains are in Nepal.
- The Nepalese flag is not rectangular – it is shaped from 2 triangles.
- Many Indian temples own elephants. The animals are decorated and used in religious festivals.

A B C D

1 2 3

China and Japan

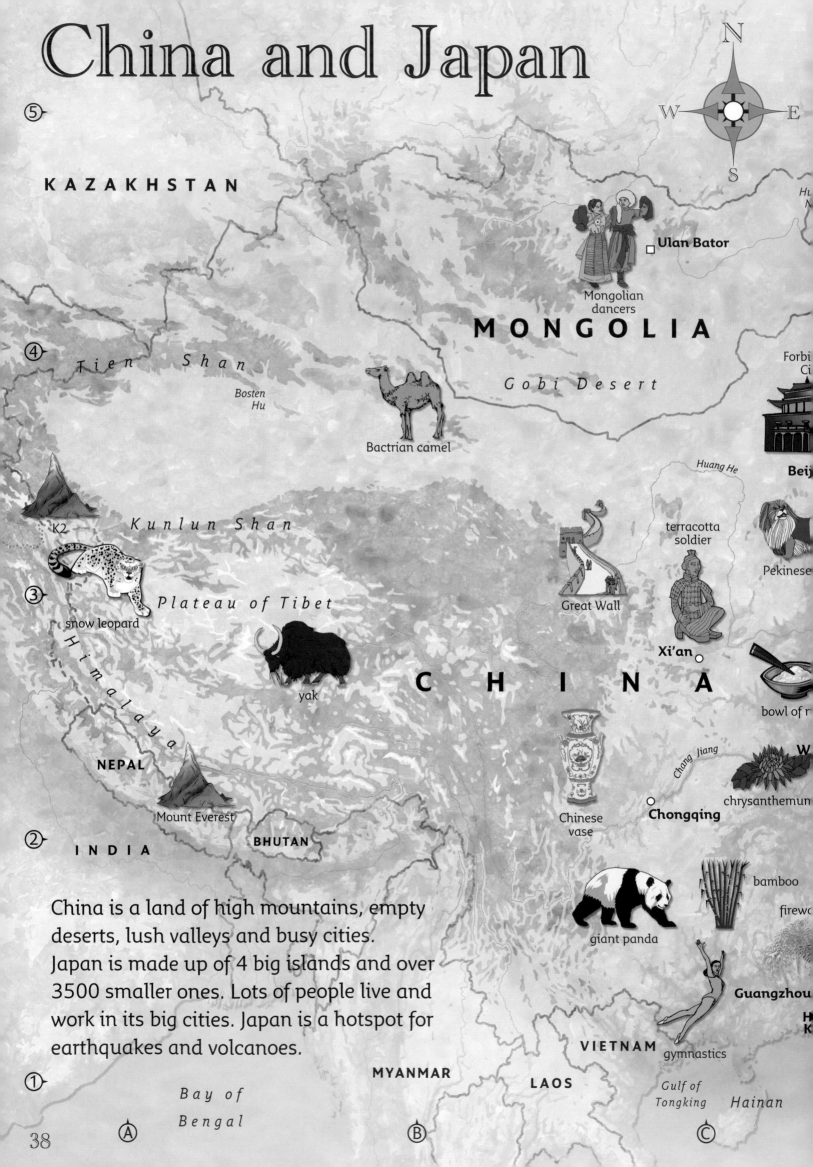

N W E S

⑤

KAZAKHSTAN

Ulan Bator

Mongolian dancers

MONGOLIA

Tien Shan

④

Bosten Hu

Gobi Desert

Bactrian camel

Forbi Ci

Huang He

③

K2

Kunlun Shan

snow leopard

Plateau of Tibet

Himalaya

Beij

terracotta soldier

Great Wall

Pekinese

Xi'an

yak

C H I N A

bowl of r

Chinese vase

Chang Jiang

Chongqing

chrysanthemum

W

NEPAL

Mount Everest

BHUTAN

② **INDIA**

China is a land of high mountains, empty deserts, lush valleys and busy cities. Japan is made up of 4 big islands and over 3500 smaller ones. Lots of people live and work in its big cities. Japan is a hotspot for earthquakes and volcanoes.

giant panda

bamboo

firewo

Guangzhou

H K

VIETNAM

gymnastics

① **MYANMAR**

LAOS

Gulf of Tongking

Hainan

Bay of Bengal

Ⓐ Ⓑ Ⓒ

RUSSIAN FEDERATION

sperm whale
Sea of Okhotsk

skiing

Sapporo

JAPAN

bonsai tree

Sea of Japan (East Sea)

karate

Harbin

kites

Shenyang

NORTH KOREA

Lake Khanka

Pyongyang

Korea Bay

Seoul

SOUTH KOREA

sumo wrestling

Tokyo

Honshu

girl in kimono

electronics industry

Yellow Sea

rickshaw

car industry

bullet train

puffer fish

Shanghai

chopsticks

East China Sea

Sakura-jima

Ryukyu Islands

Chinese junk

octopus

pagoda

Taiwan

tuna

port

Pacific Ocean

PHILIPPINES

Ⓓ   Ⓔ

Did you know?

- Gunpowder was first discovered in China. It can be used to make fireworks and signal flares.

- Chinese is spoken by almost a quarter of all the people in the world.

- China is one of the few countries where fossils of 'Big Foot' (homo gigantus) have been found.

- In Japan the green traffic light is called 'blue'.

- Japan has about 1500 earthquakes each year.

What am I?

- I am made of baked earth.

- My purpose was to protect the first Emperor in the afterlife.

- I was buried in 210-109 BC.

- I was discovered in 1974.

- I belonged to an army.

What am I?

Try this!

China has many different animals. Look at the map and find

The big furry animal who loves to eat bamboo.

Many sports are played in Japan

Can you name 2 of these?

Answers at the back of the atlas.

It's a fact

The giant panda has lived in bamboo forests for several million years. Each year a panda can eat 5 tonnes of bamboo. There are only about 1600 left in the wild.

Southeast Asia

CHINA

Taiwan Strait

Taiwan

⑤ **MYANMAR (BURMA)**

Naypyidaw

R. Irrawaddy

R. Salween

Hanoi

Buddhist monk

Hainan

satellite launch centre

Bay of Bengal

rubies

temple

L

Vientiane

python

L

Yangon (Rangoon)

THAILAND

A

O

S

R. Mekong

V
I
E
T
N
A
M

Pinatubo – vo

Ma

seafood

chili peppers

④

Angkor Wat

Bangkok

CAMBODIA

Phnom Penh

rice growing

South China Sea

Andaman Sea

scuba diving

Gulf of Thailand

Su

Se

beaches

oil rig

⑶ *Strait of Malacca*

M A L A Y S I A

BRUNEI

Bandar Seri Begawan

C

Kuala Lumpur

sky scrapers

rubber trees

Putrajaya

Sumatra tiger

Singapore

SINGAPORE

Borneo

Macassar Strait

coral reefs

Sumatra

orang utan

water bu

Ce

② *Indian Ocean*

rhinoceros

Java Sea

temple

I N D O

Jakarta

Balinese mask

Flores

Southeast Asia is made up of a tropical mainland peninsula, sometimes called Indo-China, and over 20 000 islands. Much of the region is rainforest which has a huge variety of wildlife such as elephants, tigers, orang utans and rhinoceros.

Java

volcano

Komodo dragon

surfing

①

Ⓐ

Ⓑ

Ⓒ

tuna

N
W E
S

Pacific

Ocean

t

n

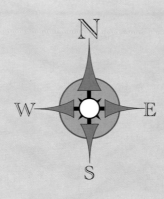
It's a fact

Many rubber tree plantations are found in Southeast Asia. When rubber trees are 5-6 years old they produce latex, collected from slits made in the tree trunk. Latex is made into rubber. The trees produce latex for 20-25 years. They are then cut down and the wood is used to make furniture.

Did you know?

- Singapore is made up of 63 islands.
- The western half of New Guinea is part of Indonesia.
- There are around 150 active volcanoes in Indonesia.
- The Sumatran tiger is the smallest tiger. It is a very fast swimmer.
- A cowrie is the shell of a snail that lives in the sea in tropical areas.

What am I?

- I am a type of lizard.
- I am only found in central Indonesia.
- I have a long body, sharp teeth and strong claws.
- My tongue is long and yellow.
- I am sometimes known as a dragon.

What am I?

Try this!

2 water sports are shown on the map. Can you name them?

Answers at the back of the atlas.

HILIPPINES

oyster and pearl

Mindanao

pineapples

s

clams

□ **Melekeok**

PALAU

manta ray

coral reefs

coconut palm tree

S I A

Banda Sea

cowrie shell

Puncak Jaya

N e w

G u i n e a

PAPUA NEW

GUINEA

rubber trees

Dili
□ **EAST TIMOR**

A r a f u r a

S e a

C o r a l

S e a

Oceania

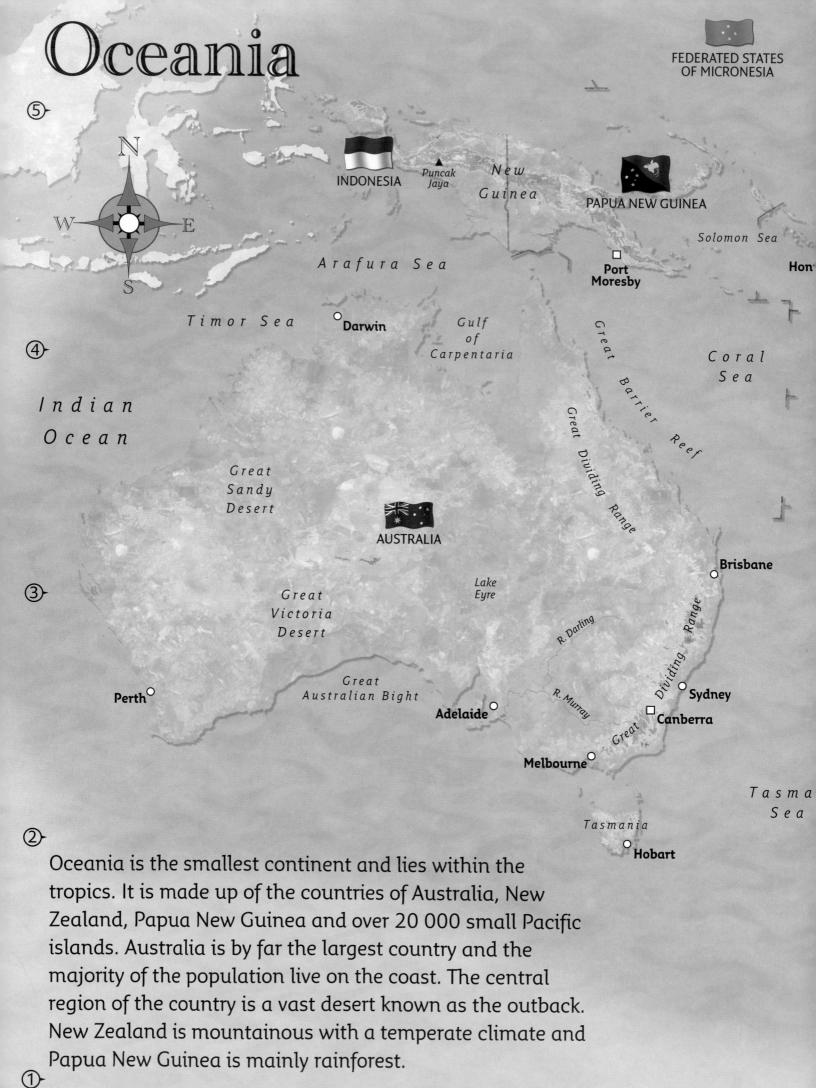

FEDERATED STATES
OF MICRONESIA

INDONESIA

*Puncak
Jaya* ▲

*New
Guinea*

PAPUA NEW GUINEA

Solomon Sea

Arafura Sea

Port
Moresby

Hon

⑤

N
W E
S

Timor Sea

Darwin

*Gulf
of
Carpentaria*

*Great
Barrier
Reef*

*Coral
Sea*

④

*Indian
Ocean*

*Great
Dividing
Range*

*Great
Sandy
Desert*

AUSTRALIA

Brisbane

③

*Lake
Eyre*

*Great
Victoria
Desert*

R. Darling

Dividing Range

R. Murray

Great

Sydney

Perth

*Great
Australian Bight*

Adelaide

Canberra

*Tasma
Sea*

Melbourne

Tasmania

② Hobart

Oceania is the smallest continent and lies within the
tropics. It is made up of the countries of Australia, New
Zealand, Papua New Guinea and over 20 000 small Pacific
islands. Australia is by far the largest country and the
majority of the population live on the coast. The central
region of the country is a vast desert known as the outback.
New Zealand is mountainous with a temperate climate and
Papua New Guinea is mainly rainforest.

①

Ⓐ

Ⓑ

Ⓒ

Bairiki □

□ Yaren

NAURU

KIRIBATI

SOLOMON
ISLANDS

TUVALU

Vaiaku
□

Wallis and
Futuna Islands
(France)

SAMOA

VANUATU

Apia □

American
Samoa
(USA)

□ Port Vila

Suva □

TONGA

Niue
(New
Zealand)

New
Caledonia
(France)   □ Nouméa

FIJI

□ Nuku'alofa

Cook
Islands
(New
Zealand)

FRENCH
POLYNESIA

Auckland ○

North
Island

P a c i f i c

O c e a n

NEW
ZEALAND

Wellington □

South
Island

Try this!

Which countries do these flags belong to?

Answers at the back of the atlas.

Did you know?

- 40% of Australia is covered by sand dunes.
- Australia's Great Barrier Reef is the world's largest coral reef.
- In South Island, New Zealand, there are 18 peaks of more than 3000 metres (9842 feet).
- The stars on the flags of Oceanic countries represent the Southern Cross constellation.
- Kangaroos are only found in Australia and New Guinea but there are over 40 different types.

People facts

- Population: 33 000 000
- Country with most people: Australia 20 155 000
- City with most people: Sydney 4 388 000

Geography facts

- Area: 8 844 516 square kilometres (3 414 887 square miles)
- Largest country: Australia 7 692 024 square kilometres (2 969 907 square miles)
- Longest river: Murray-Darling 3750 kilometres (2330 miles)
- Highest mountain: Puncak Jaya 5030 metres (16 502 feet)
- Largest lake: Lake Eyre 0-8900 square kilometres (0-3436 square miles)
- Largest island: New Guinea 808 510 square kilometres (312 167 square miles)

 D

 E

 F

Australia & New Zealand

INDONESIA

The narrow, fertile coast of eastern Australia is separated from the rest of the country by the Great Dividing Range. The highest mountain in Australia, Mount Kosciuszko, is here. New Zealand is made up of two islands. There are volcanoes on North Island. South Island has snowy mountains and glaciers.

rubber trees

New Guinea house

tree kangaroo

PAPUA NEW GUINEA

Sol

Port Moresby

④

Timor Sea

Darwin

spiny anteater

boomerang

Gulf of Carpentaria

Coral S

Great Barrier Reef

possum

scuba diving

Great Sandy Desert

frilled lizard

dingo

Great Dividing Range

koala

③

wallaby

A U S T R A L I A

kangaroo

Bris

Uluru (Ayers Rock)

Lake Eyre

Range

Australian football

emu

Great Victoria Desert

wombat

sheep

R. Darling

parakeet

Sydney Opera House

Great Dividing

Sydn

Perth

Great Australian Bight

Adelaide

cricket

R. Murray

Canberra

②

great white shark

black swan

Melbourne

Mount Kosciuszko

surfing

It's a fact

Kiwi fruit are usually the size of a hen's egg. They have hairy brown skin and bright green flesh. The fruit are named after the kiwi bird, the national bird of New Zealand. They are also known as Chinese gooseberries.

Tasmanian devils

Hobart

albatross

①

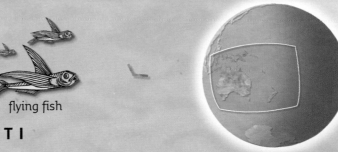

N
W • E
S

...scus

NAURU
☐ Yaren

KIRIBATI

flying fish

SOLOMON ISLANDS
Honiara ☐

clown fish

TUVALU

coconut palms

VANUATU

☐ Port Vila

bananas

New Caledonia
(France)

☐ Nouméa

octopus

Pacific Ocean

SAMOA
Apia ☐

coconuts

FIJI
☐ Suva

rugby

Nuku'alofa ☐ **TONGA**

swordfish

sea horses

What am I?

- I have powerful back legs, large feet, and use my long tail for balance.
- I like to eat grass and roots.
- I live in groups called mobs.
- As a baby, I live in my mother's pouch.
- I hop around, sometimes very fast.

What am I?

Answers at the back of the atlas.

Try this!

There are many kinds of birds and sea creatures in this region. Look at the map and find

1 black bird
4 types of sea creature

Answers at the back of the atlas.

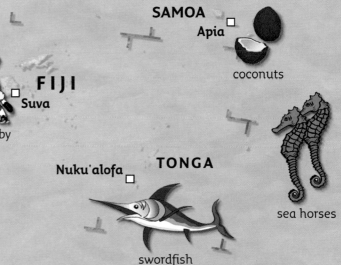

barracudas

kiwi

Auckland ○ rugby

volcanoes

Tasman Sea

kiwi fruit

☐ **Wellington**

NEW ZEALAND

sheep   takahe

Did you know?

- This region is on the opposite side of the world to Europe.
- It takes 3 days and 3 nights to cross Australia by train, from Perth to Sydney.
- On South Island, New Zealand, there are more sheep than people.
- There is natural hot steam underground on North Island. The steam is used to produce electricity.
- There are more than 850 native languages used in Papua New Guinea.

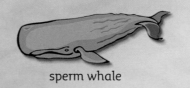

sperm whale

Ⓓ   Ⓔ   Ⓕ   45

The Arctic Ocean

The Arctic Ocean is at the North Pole. Much of the sea is covered in ice all year round. It is the smallest and shallowest ocean in the world.

Try this!

Look at the map and find

1 type of air transport
1 type of water transport
1 type of land transport

Answers at the back of the atlas.

Bering Sea

walrus

Siberian husky

Kolyma Range

polar bear

Wrangel Island

snow goose

East Siberian Sea

Siberian tiger

Brooks Range

Verkhoyansk Range

caribou

NORTH AMERICA

ice breaker ship

ski plane

ringed seal

Arctic fox

Arctic terns

Arctic Ocean

Arctic snow mobile

lynx

Arctic hare

Central Siberian Plateau

musk ox

Parry Islands

Severnaya Zemlya

North Pole

Arctic explorer

lemming

kayak

Ellesmere Island

ASIA

Baffin Island

Franz Josef Land

Kara Sea

Baffin Bay

polar bear

Arctic communications satellite

Novaya Zemlya

reindeer

ptarmigan

igloo

Spitzbergen

Barents Sea

Greenland

Inuit

killer whale

Scandinavia

Iceland

iceberg

Norwegian Sea

EUROPE

It's a fact

The Inuit are a group of people native to the coasts of the Arctic Ocean. They have lived there for over 1000 years. Inuit are hunters and fishermen. Mostly they hunt caribou and seal. Inuit fish from boats called kayaks, a type of canoe. They travel across the snow and ice on sledges pulled by teams of dogs. Their language, Inukitut, uses symbols instead of letters.

Did you know?

• The permanent ice of the Arctic Ocean is about 4 metres (13 feet) thick.

• The Arctic is the least salty of all the oceans.

• It never rains in the Arctic Ocean – it only snows.

Antarctica

Antarctica is the area of thick ice surrounding the South Pole. It is the coldest, windiest and driest continent.

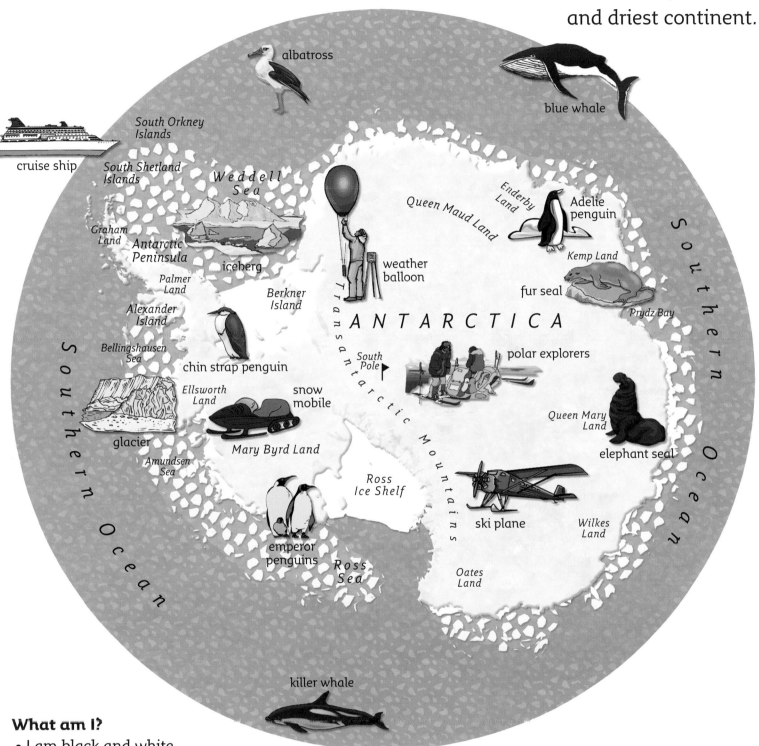

albatross

blue whale

cruise ship

South Orkney Islands

South Shetland Islands

Weddell Sea

Queen Maud Land

Enderby Land

Adelie penguin

Graham Land

Antarctic Peninsula

iceberg

Kemp Land

fur seal

Prydz Bay

Palmer Land

Berkner Island

Alexander Island

Bellingshausen Sea

chin strap penguin

Transantarctic Mountains

ANTARCTICA

South Pole

polar explorers

Queen Mary Land

elephant seal

Ellsworth Land

snow mobile

glacier

Mary Byrd Land

Amundsen Sea

Ross Ice Shelf

ski plane

Wilkes Land

emperor penguins

Ross Sea

Oates Land

Southern Ocean

Southern Ocean

killer whale

What am I?

- I am black and white.
- I eat fish and other sea life.
- I spend half my life on land and half in the sea.
- I am an excellent swimmer.
- On land I waddle on my feet, or slide on my tummy.
- I have wings but cannot fly.

What am I?

Answers at the back of the atlas.

Did you know?

- No one country owns Antarctica.
- No one lives permanently in Antarctica. Scientists visit to learn about the area.
- Many features on Antarctica are named after explorers.

Where have you been?

This world map shows some of the most visited countries in the world. You may have also visited some of these places. Perhaps you spent a holiday or visited friends and relations in these countries.

Look at the comments from children who have spent some time travelling in far away places. Would you agree with their comments or have you more interesting stories to tell?

CANADA

UNITED STATES OF AMERICA

BERMUDA

MEXICO

Barcelona

Barcelona has lots of great shops and the weather is brilliant. It has lots of beaches.

Sophie 10 years

Greece

It's really hot and has lots of outdoor swimming pools and all the times I've been there there's been some really cute cats.

Vicki 10 years

Scotland

I really like the lochs, mountains and forests. The history is definitely the best.

Jake 10 years

Australia

We built sand castles on the beach.

David 6 years

Spain

My favourite place is Salou in Spain because there is a huge theme park, Port Aventura.

Taylor 10 years

London

In London it is very cold in the winter. My Gran lives there. I love London.

Jasmin 10 years

Czech Republic

The Czech Republic is a beautiful place. I visit there with my Gran to see my cousins.

Isaac 10 years

Top 10 countries visited

1. France
2. Spain
3. United States of America
4. China
5. Italy
6. United Kingdom
7. Mexico
8. Germany
9. Turkey
10. Austria

Turkey

The food was nice, especially the lovely cherries from the market near Bodrum! We saw camels and I had a ride on one of them. The best thing was doing back flips on a bungee trampoline.

Charley 10 years

Slovakia

I really liked the snow and building a giant snowman, falling into the snow and skiing.

Marek 4 years

What do you think?

France
was in France whilst they were in the final of
the World Cup. I got to stay up late and make
as much noise as I could without being heard.
Calum 10 years

Portugal
I like the
swimming
pools outside.
Cain 10 years

France
I used to live in
France. I will
always have this
memory. One day
it went snowy, sun,
snow, sun etc....
**Cameron
10 years**

GERMANY
UNITED
KINGDOM
CZECH
REP.
ELAND
SLOVAKIA
FRANCE
AUSTRIA
ITALY
TUGAL
TURKEY
SPAIN
GREECE

CHINA

INDIA

Scotland
The most exciting thing
was when I was panning
for gold at the Wanlockhead
Lead Mine Museum and found
some in the bottom of my pan.
Callum 8 years

MALAYSIA

KENYA

SOUTH
AFRICA

AUSTRALIA

NEW
ZEALAND

Florida
We went to Disneyworld
to see Mickey Mouse.
It was very hot.
Brad 7 years

Majorca
It is famous because
it has a Pirate Show.
Its main place is Palma.
Ross 10 years

Scotland
My favourite place
is Loch Lomond.
Jordan 10 years

Scotland
I went to Millport. It was thunder
and lightning. It struck a lamppost
and it fell down on the road.
Antonio 10 years

Scotland
Edinburgh Dungeons has
the most scary weirdest
monsters in the world.
I got the monster stuck
in my dreams.
Brian 10 years

Disneyland Paris
Disneyland was great.
It was sad when I
had to leave.
Daniel 10 years

Spain
I liked Majorca because of the sun and
the price of shopping. It was also really
good because of the big beaches.
Kieran 10 years

Where have you been?

There are many reasons to travel to far away places. The symbols around this map show a selection of these. Names on the map tell us some of the best places to visit.

More interesting stories are also shown.

Sightseeing

Beach holiday

North America

Rocky Mountains

Winter sports

Bird watching

Caribbean Sea   Cruise

South America

Andes

Desert S

USA

I like Universal Studio because it has fantastic rides. I would give it a ten out of ten.

Sam 10 years

Kenya

We were in a big car and saw elephants and lions. I liked the lions but they had big teeth. It was very dusty and hot.

Katie 7 years

USA

I used to live in Vermont. In winter it snows a lot and in the summer it is very hot.

Aidan 10 years

India

India is the greatest place ever.

Naomi 10 years

Malaysia

We went to the jungle and saw lots of animals in the trees. I was scared because the animals made lots of noise at night. It was hot but it rained every day.

Kim 8 years

Exploring

A n

Australia

I love Australia because of all the different animals on land and in the water and all of the lovely weather.

Robbie 10 years

Canary Islands

My favourite place is Tenerife because it's very comfortable…

Darren 10 years

Cadiz, Spain

My feet were almost burnt when I went on the beaches because the sand was so hot. Luckily the water cooled me down.

Helen 10 years

What do you think?

Turkey

't's really HOT!! I sleep walked into the hallway
of our dormitory and I had nightmares about
one of my Aunt's friend's cousins.

Sean 10 years

Scotland

Arran is an island off the southwest coast of Scotland.
The funniest thing is when my friend catapults people
across the bedroom with his feet. The best thing was
when I got to ride a horse through a river on a pony trek.

Rona 10 years

South Africa

It was hot. We went on a boat
and saw fish in the sea. I had
a sore tummy in the boat.

Cameron 5 years

Greece

Rhodes in Greece is quiet with
fantastic beaches.

Martha 10 years

Asia

Himalaya

n Sea

a

frica

East
Africa

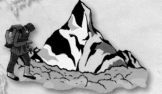

Trekking

Spain

My favourite city is
Barcelona because it
is very lively.

Megan 10 years

Australia

Water sports

Wildlife watching

New Zealand

We made snowballs to
throw at each other.
But it was very cold.

Sophie 8 years

t i c a

Canada

I love Canada because of the cool
stuff to see and it is only 1 hour
away from Disneyland.

Makeila 10 years

Ireland

My Great Granny lives in Ireland.
It has great restaurants.

Molly 10 years

Barcelona

Barcelona has lots
of great shops and
the weather is
brilliant. It has lots
of beaches.

Sophie 10 years

USA

Florida is where I always go with my family.
There are lots of things to do like rides and stuff.

Megan 10 years

Bermuda

Bermuda is always peaceful
and quiet.

Callum 10 years

51

Countries of the World

	COUNTRY, CONTINENT / Capital City / Population	Area square kilometres (square miles)
Flag		

Flag	Country / Capital / Population	Area
	AFGHANISTAN, ASIA — Kabul — 29 863 000	652 225 (251 825)
	ALBANIA, EUROPE — Tirana — 3 130 000	28 748 (11 100)
	ALGERIA, AFRICA — Algiers — 32 854 000	2 381 741 (919 595)
	ANGOLA, AFRICA — Luanda — 15 941 000	1 246 700 (481 353)
	ARGENTINA, SOUTH AMERICA — Buenos Aires — 38 747 000	2 766 889 (1 068 302)
	ARMENIA, ASIA — Yerevan — 3 016 000	29 800 (11 506)
	AUSTRALIA, OCEANIA — Canberra — 20 155 000	7 692 024 (2 969 907)
	AUSTRIA, EUROPE — Vienna — 8 189 000	83 855 (32 377)
	BAHRAIN, ASIA — Manama — 727 000	691 (267)
	BANGLADESH, ASIA — Dhaka — 141 822 000	143 998 (55 598)
	BELARUS, EUROPE — Minsk — 9 755 000	207 600 (80 155)
	BELGIUM, EUROPE — Brussels — 10 419 000	30 520 (11 784)
	BENIN, AFRICA — Porto Novo — 8 439 000	112 620 (43 483)
	BHUTAN, ASIA — Thimphu — 2 163 000	46 620 (18 000)
	BOLIVIA, SOUTH AMERICA — La Paz/Sucre — 9 182 000	1 098 581 (424 164)
	BOSNIA-HERZEGOVINA, EUROPE — Sarajevo — 3 907 000	51 130 (19 741)
	BOTSWANA, AFRICA — Gaborone — 1 765 000	581 370 (224 468)
	BRAZIL, SOUTH AMERICA — Brasília — 186 405 000	8 514 879 (3 287 613)
	BRUNEI, ASIA — Bandar Seri Begawan — 374 000	5 765 (2 226)
	BULGARIA, EUROPE — Sofia — 7 726 000	110 994 (42 855)
	BURKINA, AFRICA — Ouagadougou — 13 228 000	274 200 (105 869)
	BURUNDI, AFRICA — Bujumbura — 7 548 000	27 835 (10 747)
	CAMBODIA, ASIA — Phnom Penh — 14 071 000	181 035 (69 884)
	CAMEROON, AFRICA — Yaoundé — 16 322 000	475 442 (183 569)
	CANADA, NORTH AMERICA — Ottawa — 32 268 000	9 984 670 (3 855 103)
	CENTRAL AFRICAN REPUBLIC, AFRICA — Bangui — 4 038 000	622 436 (240 324)
	CHAD, AFRICA — Ndjamena — 9 749 000	1 284 000 (495 755)
	CHILE, SOUTH AMERICA — Santiago — 16 295 000	756 945 (292 258)
	CHINA, ASIA — Beijing — 1 323 345 000	9 620 671 (3 714 562)
	COLOMBIA, SOUTH AMERICA — Bogotá — 45 600 000	1 141 748 (440 831)
	CONGO, AFRICA — Brazzaville — 3 999 000	342 000 (132 047)
	CONGO, DEMOCRATIC REPUBLIC OF THE AFRICA — Kinshasa — 57 549 000	2 345 410 (905 568)
	COSTA RICA, NORTH AMERICA — San José — 4 327 000	51 100 (19 730)
	CÔTE D'IVOIRE, AFRICA — Yamoussoukro — 18 154 000	322 463 (124 504)
	CROATIA, EUROPE — Zagreb — 4 551 000	56 538 (21 829)
	CUBA, NORTH AMERICA — Havana — 11 269 000	110 860 (42 803)
	CYPRUS, ASIA — Nicosia — 835 000	9 251 (3 572)
	CZECH REPUBLIC, EUROPE — Prague — 10 220 000	78 864 (30 450)
	DENMARK, EUROPE — Copenhagen — 5 431 000	43 075 (16 631)

DJIBOUTI, AFRICA
Djibouti
793 000
23 200
(8 958)

DOMINICAN REPUBLIC, NORTH AMERICA
Santo Domingo
8 895 000
48 442
(18 704)

EAST TIMOR, ASIA
Dili
947 000
14 874
(5 743)

ECUADOR, SOUTH AMERICA
Quito
13 228 000
272 045
(105 037)

EGYPT, AFRICA
Cairo
74 033 000
1 000 250
(386 199)

EL SALVADOR, NORTH AMERICA
San Salvador
6 881 000
21 041
(8 124)

EQUATORIAL GUINEA, AFRICA
Malabo
504 000
28 051
(10 831)

ERITREA, AFRICA
Asmara
4 401 000
117 400
(45 328)

ESTONIA, EUROPE
Tallinn
1 330 000
45 200
(17 452)

ETHIOPIA, AFRICA
Addis Ababa
77 431 000
1 133 880
(437 794)

FINLAND, EUROPE
Helsinki
5 249 000
338 145
(130 559)

FRANCE, EUROPE
Paris
60 496 000
543 965
(210 026)

GABON, AFRICA
Libreville
1 384 000
267 667
(103 347)

GEORGIA, ASIA
T'bilisi
4 474 000
69 700
(26 911)

GERMANY, EUROPE
Berlin
82 689 000
357 022
(137 849)

GHANA, AFRICA
Accra
22 113 000
238 537
(92 100)

GREECE, EUROPE
Athens
11 120 000
131 957
(50 949)

GUATEMALA, NORTH AMERICA
Guatemala City
12 599 000
108 890
(42 043)

GUINEA, AFRICA
Conakry
6 402 000
245 857
(94 926)

GUINEA-BISSAU, AFRICA
Bissau
1 586 000
36 125
(13 948)

GUYANA, SOUTH AMERICA
Georgetown
751 000
214 969
(83 000)

HAITI, NORTH AMERICA
Port-au-Prince
8 528 000
27 750
(10 714)

HONDURAS, NORTH AMERICA
Tegucigalpa
7 205 000
112 088
(43 277)

HUNGARY, EUROPE
Budapest
10 098 000
93 030
(35 919)

ICELAND, EUROPE
Reykjavik
295 000
102 820
(39 699)

INDIA, ASIA
New Delhi
1 103 371 000
3 064 898
(1 183 364)

INDONESIA, ASIA
Jakarta
222 781 000
1 919 445
(741 102)

IRAN, ASIA
Tehran
69 515 000
1 648 000
(636 296)

IRAQ, ASIA
Baghdad
28 807 000
438 317
(169 235)

IRELAND EUROPE
Dublin
4 148 000
70 282
(27 136)

ISRAEL, ASIA
Jerusalem
6 725 000
20 770
(8 019)

ITALY, EUROPE
Rome
58 093 000
301 245
(116 311)

JAMAICA, NORTH AMERICA
Kingston
2 651 000
10 991
(4 244)

JAPAN, ASIA
Tokyo
128 085 000
377 727
(145 841)

JORDAN, ASIA
Amman
5 703 000
89 206
(34 443)

KAZAKHSTAN, ASIA
Astana
14 825 000
2 717 300
(1 049 155)

KENYA, AFRICA
Nairobi
34 256 000
582 646
(224 961)

KUWAIT, ASIA
Kuwait
2 687 000
17 818
(6 880)

KYRGYZSTAN, ASIA
Bishkek
5 264 000
198 500
(76 641)

LAOS, ASIA
Vientiane
5 924 000
236 800
(91 429)

Countries of the World

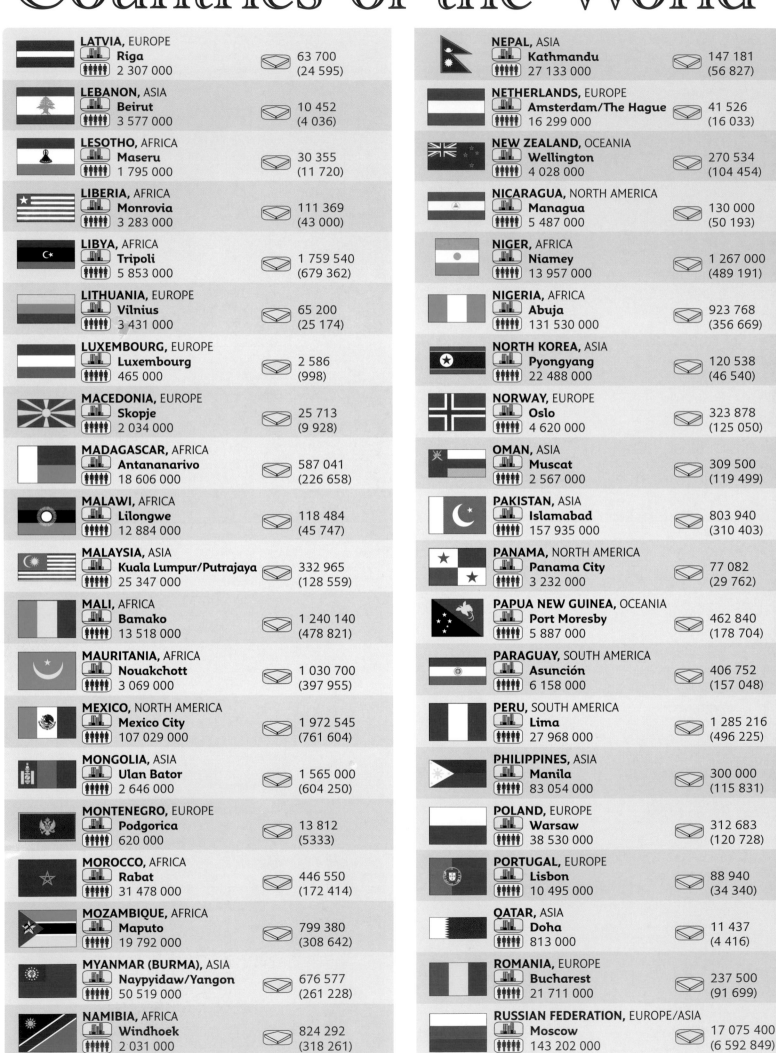

LATVIA, EUROPE
Riga
2 307 000
63 700
(24 595)

LEBANON, ASIA
Beirut
3 577 000
10 452
(4 036)

LESOTHO, AFRICA
Maseru
1 795 000
30 355
(11 720)

LIBERIA, AFRICA
Monrovia
3 283 000
111 369
(43 000)

LIBYA, AFRICA
Tripoli
5 853 000
1 759 540
(679 362)

LITHUANIA, EUROPE
Vilnius
3 431 000
65 200
(25 174)

LUXEMBOURG, EUROPE
Luxembourg
465 000
2 586
(998)

MACEDONIA, EUROPE
Skopje
2 034 000
25 713
(9 928)

MADAGASCAR, AFRICA
Antananarivo
18 606 000
587 041
(226 658)

MALAWI, AFRICA
Lilongwe
12 884 000
118 484
(45 747)

MALAYSIA, ASIA
Kuala Lumpur/Putrajaya
25 347 000
332 965
(128 559)

MALI, AFRICA
Bamako
13 518 000
1 240 140
(478 821)

MAURITANIA, AFRICA
Nouakchott
3 069 000
1 030 700
(397 955)

MEXICO, NORTH AMERICA
Mexico City
107 029 000
1 972 545
(761 604)

MONGOLIA, ASIA
Ulan Bator
2 646 000
1 565 000
(604 250)

MONTENEGRO, EUROPE
Podgorica
620 000
13 812
(5333)

MOROCCO, AFRICA
Rabat
31 478 000
446 550
(172 414)

MOZAMBIQUE, AFRICA
Maputo
19 792 000
799 380
(308 642)

MYANMAR (BURMA), ASIA
Naypyidaw/Yangon
50 519 000
676 577
(261 228)

NAMIBIA, AFRICA
Windhoek
2 031 000
824 292
(318 261)

NEPAL, ASIA
Kathmandu
27 133 000
147 181
(56 827)

NETHERLANDS, EUROPE
Amsterdam/The Hague
16 299 000
41 526
(16 033)

NEW ZEALAND, OCEANIA
Wellington
4 028 000
270 534
(104 454)

NICARAGUA, NORTH AMERICA
Managua
5 487 000
130 000
(50 193)

NIGER, AFRICA
Niamey
13 957 000
1 267 000
(489 191)

NIGERIA, AFRICA
Abuja
131 530 000
923 768
(356 669)

NORTH KOREA, ASIA
Pyongyang
22 488 000
120 538
(46 540)

NORWAY, EUROPE
Oslo
4 620 000
323 878
(125 050)

OMAN, ASIA
Muscat
2 567 000
309 500
(119 499)

PAKISTAN, ASIA
Islamabad
157 935 000
803 940
(310 403)

PANAMA, NORTH AMERICA
Panama City
3 232 000
77 082
(29 762)

PAPUA NEW GUINEA, OCEANIA
Port Moresby
5 887 000
462 840
(178 704)

PARAGUAY, SOUTH AMERICA
Asunción
6 158 000
406 752
(157 048)

PERU, SOUTH AMERICA
Lima
27 968 000
1 285 216
(496 225)

PHILIPPINES, ASIA
Manila
83 054 000
300 000
(115 831)

POLAND, EUROPE
Warsaw
38 530 000
312 683
(120 728)

PORTUGAL, EUROPE
Lisbon
10 495 000
88 940
(34 340)

QATAR, ASIA
Doha
813 000
11 437
(4 416)

ROMANIA, EUROPE
Bucharest
21 711 000
237 500
(91 699)

RUSSIAN FEDERATION, EUROPE/ASIA
Moscow
143 202 000
17 075 400
(6 592 849)

SAUDI ARABIA, ASIA
Riyadh
24 573 000
2 200 000
(849 425)

SENEGAL, AFRICA
Dakar
11 658 000
196 720
(75 954)

SERBIA, EUROPE
Belgrade
9 379 000
88 361
(34 116)

SIERRA LEONE, AFRICA
Freetown
5 525 000
71 740
(27 699)

SINGAPORE, ASIA
Singapore
4 326 000
639
(247)

SLOVAKIA, EUROPE
Bratislava
5 401 000
49 035
(18 933)

SLOVENIA, EUROPE
Ljubljana
1 967 000
20 251
(7 819)

SOMALIA, AFRICA
Mogadishu
8 228 000
637 657
(246 201)

SOUTH AFRICA, REPUBLIC OF AFRICA
Pretoria/Cape Town
47 432 000
1 219 090
(470 693)

SOUTH KOREA, ASIA
Seoul
47 817 000
99 274
(38 330)

SOUTH SUDAN, AFRICA
Juba
8 260 490
644 329
(248 777)

SPAIN, EUROPE
Madrid
43 064 000
504 782
(194 897)

SRI LANKA, ASIA
Sri Jayewardenepura Kotte
20 743 000
65 610
(25 332)

SUDAN, AFRICA
Khartoum
36 233 000
1 861 484
(718 723)

SURINAME, SOUTH AMERICA
Paramaribo
449 000
163 820
(63 251)

SWAZILAND, AFRICA
Mbabane
1 032 000
17 364
(6 704)

SWEDEN, EUROPE
Stockholm
9 041 000
449 964
(173 732)

SWITZERLAND, EUROPE
Bern
7 252 000
41 293
(15 943)

SYRIA, ASIA
Damascus
19 043 000
185 180
(71 498)

TAJIKISTAN, ASIA
Dushanbe
6 507 000
143 100
(55 251)

TANZANIA, AFRICA
Dodoma
38 329 000
945 087
(364 900)

THAILAND, ASIA
Bangkok
64 233 000
513 115
(198 115)

THE GAMBIA, AFRICA
Banjul
1 517 000
11 295
(4 361)

TOGO, AFRICA
Lomé
6 145 000
56 785
(21 925)

TRINIDAD AND TOBAGO, NORTH AMERICA
Port of Spain
1 305 000
5 130
(1 981)

TUNISIA, AFRICA
Tunis
10 102 000
164 150
(63 379)

TURKEY, ASIA/EUROPE
Ankara
73 193 000
779 452
(300 948)

TURKMENISTAN, ASIA
Ashgabat
4 833 000
488 100
(188 456)

UGANDA, AFRICA
Kampala
28 816 000
241 038
(93 065)

UKRAINE, EUROPE
Kiev
46 481 000
603 700
(233 090)

UNITED ARAB EMIRATES, ASIA
Abu Dhabi
4 496 000
77 700
(30 000)

UNITED KINGDOM, EUROPE
London
59 668 000
243 609
(94 058)

UNITED STATES OF AMERICA, NORTH AMERICA
Washington
298 213 000
9 826 635
(3 794 085)

URUGUAY, SOUTH AMERICA
Montevideo
3 463 000
176 215
(68 037)

UZBEKISTAN, ASIA
Tashkent
26 593 000
447 400
(172 742)

VENEZUELA, SOUTH AMERICA
Caracas
26 749 000
912 050
(352 144)

VIETNAM, ASIA
Hanoi
84 238 000
329 565
(127 246)

YEMEN, ASIA
San'a
20 975 000
527 968
(203 850)

ZAMBIA, AFRICA
Lusaka
11 668 000
752 614
(290 586)

ZIMBABWE, AFRICA
Harare
13 010 000
390 759
(150 873)

55

Games and Quizzes

Name the continents
Match the numbers on the map to the continent names listed.

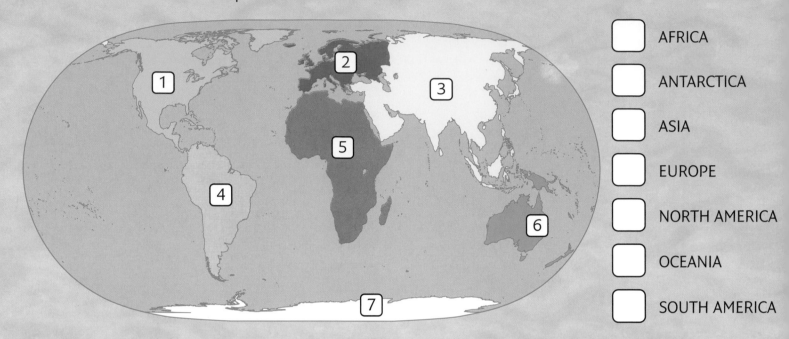

AFRICA

ANTARCTICA

ASIA

EUROPE

NORTH AMERICA

OCEANIA

SOUTH AMERICA

Name the countries
Match the shapes to the country names listed.

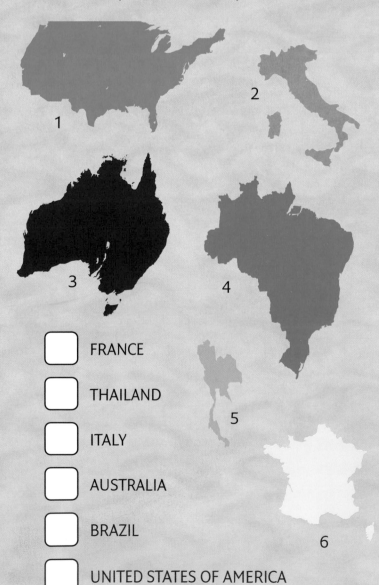

FRANCE

THAILAND

ITALY

AUSTRALIA

BRAZIL

UNITED STATES OF AMERICA

Search for cities
The 12 capital cities listed below are hidden in this grid. See how many you can find.

A	O	W	E	L	L	I	N	G	T	O	N
B	P	X	Z	P	O	J	X	Z	Q	J	O
W	A	S	H	I	N	G	T	O	N	V	T
X	R	K	Y	Y	D	W	V	J	F	X	T
C	I	K	P	F	O	X	Z	Q	J	F	A
A	S	Z	B	A	N	G	K	O	K	X	W
N	J	V	Q	Z	X	X	C	H	Z	Y	A
B	R	A	S	I	L	I	A	W	X	T	V
E	W	H	G	M	X	Z	I	Z	F	U	X
R	O	M	E	X	Q	V	R	J	Q	N	F
R	V	W	T	O	K	Y	O	V	W	I	Q
A	Q	W	H	G	M	X	T	J	V	S	Q

LONDON   WELLINGTON   CAIRO
PARIS   TOKYO   TUNIS
ROME   BANGKOK   OTTAWA
CANBERRA   BRASILIA   WASHINGTON

Quiz 1
1. What is the largest country in the world?

2. What is the capital of France?

3. How many stars are on the flag of China?

Colour match

All these symbols have a colour in part of their name. Find their correct name by matching a colour with one of the other words.

1. _ _ _ _ _ _ _   _ _ _ _ _

2. _ _ _ _   _ _ _ _ _ _ _ _

3. _ _ _ _ _   _ _ _ _

4. _ _ _ _ _ _ _ _ _ _ _

5. _ _ _ _ _   _ _ _ _ _   _ _ _ _ _

blue	flamingo
brown	berries
pink	shark
purple	bear
great white	finch

Unscramble the countries

Rearrange the letters in the boxes to find the names of 6 countries.

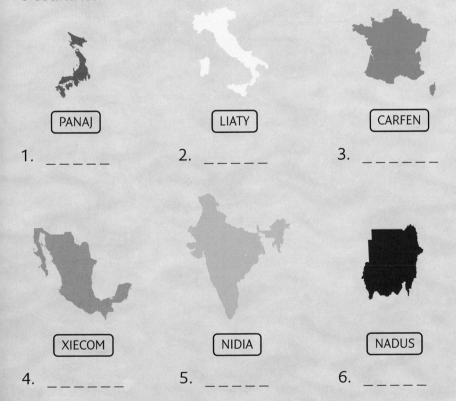

PANAJ
1. _ _ _ _ _

LIATY
2. _ _ _ _ _

CARFEN
3. _ _ _ _ _ _

XIECOM
4. _ _ _ _ _ _

NIDIA
5. _ _ _ _ _

NADUS
6. _ _ _ _ _

Quiz 2

1. What is the world's longest river?

2. How many colours are on the flag of Italy?

3. What kind of bears are found in Arctic regions?

Whose flag is this?

There are 16 country flags and 16 country names shown below. Try to match up the country names to their flag. Add the correct flag number to the box beside each country name.

1. 🇨🇦   2. 🇦🇺
3. 🇬🇷   4. 🇺🇸
5. 🇵🇰   6. 🇩🇰
7. 🇧🇷   8.
9. 🇨🇳   10. 🇬🇧
11. 🇳🇿   12. 🇯🇵
13. 🇳🇵   14. 🇨🇱
15. 🇿🇦   16.

☐ CHINA	☐ JAPAN
☐ CANADA	☐ GREECE
☐ PAKISTAN	☐ NEPAL
☐ BRAZIL	☐ SOMALIA
☐ CHILE	☐ SWEDEN
☐ AUSTRALIA	☐ KENYA

☐ NEW ZEALAND

☐ UNITED KINGDOM

☐ REPUBLIC OF SOUTH AFRICA

☐ UNITED STATES OF AMERICA

Answers on page 64.

57

Games and Quizzes

Name the oceans

Match the numbers on the map to the ocean names listed.

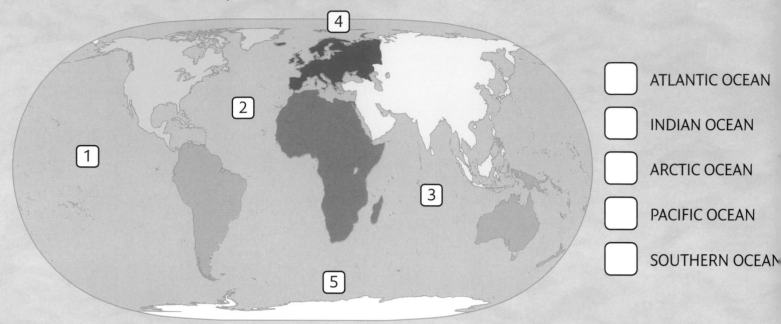

☐ ATLANTIC OCEAN

☐ INDIAN OCEAN

☐ ARCTIC OCEAN

☐ PACIFIC OCEAN

☐ SOUTHERN OCEAN

Name the symbol

Choose a suitable caption for each symbol from the names in the panel on the right.
Only one caption will match each symbol.

1. _____   2. _____

Puffin	Kiwi fruit	Owl
	Bobcat	Polar bear
Grapes	Taj Mahal	
Stonehenge	Hockey	Apple
	Banana	Cricket
Walrus		
Oil platform	Shamrock	
	Sydney Opera House	

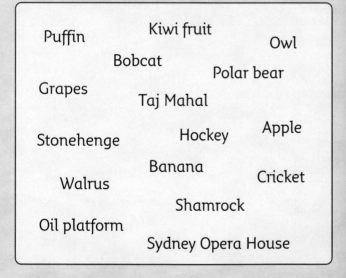

3. _____   4. _____

5. _____   6. _____

Quiz 3

1. What is the capital of Argentina?

2. How many blue stripes appear on the flag of Honduras?

3. In which country would you watch this sport?

Symbol Match

In which country would you expect to see these?
Add the correct symbol number to the box beside each country name.

1. Tower Bridge

2. Croissants

3. Liberty Bell

4. Taj Mahal

5. Kangaroo

6. Zulu house

☐ UNITED STATES OF AMERICA   ☐ FRANCE

☐ UNITED KINGDOM   ☐ SWAZILAND

☐ INDIA   ☐ AUSTRALIA

Which continent are you in?

Look at the groups of flags below.
Which continent would you be in if these flags were shown?

1.

2.

3.

4.

5.

6.

☐ ASIA   ☐ OCEANIA

☐ EUROPE   ☐ NORTH AMERICA

☐ SOUTH AMERICA   ☐ AFRICA

Search for countries

The 10 countries listed below
are hidden in this grid.
See how many you can find.

A	R	G	E	N	T	I	N	A	F	K	Y
N	V	G	F	Y	N	E	Z	U	Z	B	V
C	Y	D	Q	C	G	G	G	S	X	Q	J
H	U	N	G	A	R	Y	B	T	G	B	J
I	L	A	F	N	G	P	H	R	B	O	Q
N	N	L	Z	A	S	T	V	A	P	T	X
A	G	O	X	D	T	V	F	L	H	S	F
H	P	O	L	A	N	D	Z	I	H	W	F
H	Y	X	Q	Q	V	Z	X	A	Z	A	O
M	E	X	I	C	O	G	G	V	G	N	Q
Q	Z	J	B	Y	F	F	B	X	B	A	J
N	I	G	E	R	I	A	B	J	Q	K	P

ARGENTINA

AUSTRALIA

BOTSWANA

CANADA

CHINA

EGYPT

HUNGARY

MEXICO

NIGERIA

POLAND

Quiz 4

1. What is the world's highest mountain?

2. What is the capital of China?

3. In which country would you find these animals?

Answers on page 64.

Index

This index lists all the important place names shown on the maps. The grid code numbers and letters help you to find the correct position of the name on each map.

Gran Chaco 14 B5
Great Australian Bight
 44 B2
Great Barrier Reef 44 C4
Great Dividing Range 44 C3
Great Rift Valley 20 C5
Great Sandy Desert 44 A3
Great Victoria Desert 44 B2
Greece 29 D2
Greenland 5 D5
Grenada 9 F2
Guadalajara 8 B3
Guadeloupe 9 F3
Guatemala 8 C2
Guatemala City 8 C2
Guayaquil 12 A2
Guiana Highlands 12 C3
Guinea 18 B2
Guinea Bissau 18 B3
Gulf of Aden 19 F3
Gulf of Alaska 4 A4
Gulf of California 8 A5
Gulf of Guinea 18 C2
Gulf of Mexico 8 C4
Gulf of Oman 34 C1
Guyana 12 C3

H

Haiti 9 E3
Hamburg 28 C5
Hannover 28 C5
Hanoi 40 B5
Harare 21 C4
Havana 9 D3
Helsinki 27 E3
Himalaya 36 B5
Hindu Kush 35 F4
Honduras 8 C2
Hong Kong 38 C1
Honiara 45 D4
Houston 6 C2
Hudson Bay 5 D2
Hungary 27 D1
Hyderabad 37 B3

I

Iceland 26 B5
India 37 B4
Indian Ocean 20 D5
Indonesia 40 C2
Indore 37 B4
Indus 35 F4
Inverness 24 C5
Iguacu Falls 14 C5
Iran 35 D4
Iraq 34 C3
Ireland 25 A3
Irish Sea 25 B3
Irkutsk 33 D2
Irrawaddy 37 D3
Irtysh 32 B2
Islamabad 36 B5
Isle of Man 25 B3
Israel 34 B4
Istanbul 29 E3
Italy 28 C3

J

Jaipur 36 B4
Jakarta 40 B2
Jamaica 9 D3
Japan 39 D4
Java 40 B2
Java Sea 40 B2
Jerusalem 34 B4
Johannesburg 21 C3
Jordan 34 C4
Juba 19 E2

K

K2 38 A3
Kabul 35 F4
Kalahari Desert 21 B3
Kamchatka Peninsula 33 E4
Kampala 20 C5
Kansas City 6 C3
Karachi 37 A4
Karakoram Range 35 F4
Kathmandu 36 C5
Kazakhstan 32 B2
Kenya 20 C6
Khabarovsk 33 E2
Khartoum 19 E3
Kiev 29 E5
Kigali 20 C5
Kilimanjaro 20 C5
Kingston 9 D3
Kinshasa 20 B5
Kiribati 45 E5
Kolkata 37 D4
Kosovo 29 D3
Krasnoyarsk 32 C2
Kuala Lumpur 40 B3
Kunlun Shan 38 A3
Kuwait 35 D3
Kuwait (city) 35 D3
Kyrgyzstan 32 B1

L

Laayoune 18 B4
Lagos 18 C2
Lahore 36 B5
Lake Baikal 33 D2
Lake Balkhash 32 B2
Lake Chad 19 D3
Lake Erie 7 D4
Lake Huron 7 D4
Lake Lagoda 27 E4
Lake Michigan 7 D4
Lake Nicaragua 9 D2
Lake Nyasa 20 C4
Lake Onega 27 E4
Lake Ontario 7 E4
Lake Superior 7 D4
Lake Tanganyika 20 C5
Lake Titicaca 14 A6
Lake Turkana 20 C6
Lake Victoria 20 C5
Laos 40 B5
La Paz 14 A6
Lappland 27 D5
Las Vegas 6 A3
Latvia 27 E3

Lebanon 34 B4
Leeds 25 C3
Lena 33 D3
Lesotho 21 C3
Liberia 18 B2
Libreville 20 A5
Libya 19 D4
Liechtenstein 28 C4
Lilongwe 20 C4
Lima 12 A1
Limerick 25 A3
Limpopo 21 C3
Lisbon 28 A3
Lithuania 27 E2
Liverpool 25 C3
Ljubljana 29 D4
Lomé 18 C2
London 25 D2
Londonderry 25 B4
Los Angeles 6 A3
Lough Neagh 25 B4
Luanda 20 A5
Lubumbashi 20 C4
Lusaka 21 C4
Luxembourg 26 C1
Luxembourg (city) 26 C1
Luzon 40 D5

M

Macedonia 29 D3
Madagascar 21 D3
Madeira 12 C2
Madrid 28 B3
Malabo 18 C2
Malawi 20 C4
Malaysia 40 B3
Maldives 37 B1
Mali 18 C3
Malta 29 D2
Managua 9 D2
Manama 35 D3
Manaus 12 C2
Manchester 25 C3
Mandalay 37 D4
Manila 40 C4
Maputo 21 C3
Maracaibo 12 B4
Marseille 28 C3
Martinique 9 F3
Maseru 21 C3
Massif Central 28 B4
Mauritania 18 B3
Mauritius 17 D3
Mbabane 21 C3
Medellín 12 B3
Mediterranean Sea 28 C2
Melbourne 44 C2
Melekeok 41 E3
Mendoza 15 B4
Mexico 8 B4
Mexico City 8 B3
Miami 7 E1
Middlesbrough 24 C4
Milan 28 C3
Mindanao 41 D3
Minneapolis 6 C4
Minsk 27 E2
Missouri 6 B5
Mogadishu 20 D6

Moldova 29 E4
Monaco 28 C3
Mongolia 38 B4
Monrovia 18 B2
Montenegro 29 D3
Monterrey 8 B4
Montevideo 15 C3
Montréal 5 D1
Montserrat 9 F3
Morocco 18 B4
Moscow 32 A3
Mount Everest 36 C4
Mount Logan 4 B3
Mount McKinley 4 A4
Mount Rainer 6 A4
Mozambique 21 C3
Mumbai 37 B3
Munich 28 C4
Murray 44 C2
Muscat 35 E2
Myanmar (Burma) 40 A5

N

Nagpur 37 C3
Nairobi 20 C5
Namib Desert 21 B3
Namibia 21 B4
Nassau 9 D4
Nauru 45 D5
Naypyidaw 40 A5
Ndjamena 19 D2
Negro 12 C3
Nepal 36 C5
Netherlands 26 C2
New Caledonia 45 D3
Newcastle upon Tyne
 25 C4
New Delhi 36 B5
New Guinea 41 E2
New Orleans 7 D2
New York 7 E4
New Zealand 45 E1
Niagara Falls 5 D1
Niamey 18 C3
Nicaragua 9 D2
Nicosia 34 B4
Niger 18 C3
Nigeria 18 C2
Nile 19 E4
North America 2-3
Northern Ireland 25 B4
North Korea 39 D4
North Sea 24 C4
Norway 26 C3
Nouakchott 18 B3
Nouméa 45 D3
Novosibirsk 32 C2
Nuku'alofa 45 F3
Nuuk (Godthåb) 5 E3

O

Ob 32 B3
Oceania 42 -43
Oman 35 D2
Omsk 32 B2
Oporto 28 A3
Orange 21 B3
Orinoco 12 C4

Orkney Islands 24 C6
Oslo 27 D3
Ottawa 5 D1
Ougadougou 18 C3
Outer Hebrides 24 B5

P

Pacific Ocean 4 A3
Pakistan 35 E3
Palau 41 E3
Panama 9 D2
Panama Canal 9 D2
Panama City 9 D2
Papua New Guinea 44 C5
Paraguay 14 B5
Paramaribo 13 D3
Paraná 14 C5
Paris 28 B4
Patagonia 15 A1
Patna 36 C4
Pechora 32 B4
Perm 32 B3
Perth 44 A2
Peru 12 B1
Philadelphia 7 E3
Philippines 41 D4
Phnom Penh 40 B4
Phoenix 6 B2
Pittsburgh 7 E3
Planalto do Mato Grosso
  14 C7
Plateau of Tibet 38 A3
Po 28 C3
Podgorica 29 D3
Poland 27 D2
Port-au-Prince 9 E3
Port Moresby 44 C4
Porto Alegre 14 C4
Porto-Novo 18 C2
Portsmouth 25 C1
Portugal 28 A3
Port Vila 45 E3
Prague 27 D1
Praia 18 A3
Pretoria (Tshwane) 21 C3
Priština 29 D3
Puerto Rico 9 F3
Puncak Jaya 41 E2
Putrajaya 40 B3
Pyongyang 39 D4
Pyrenees 28 B3

Q

Qatar 35 D3
Québec 5 E1
Quito 12 A3

R

Rabat 18 C5
Ras Dejen 19 F3
Recife 13 F1
Red Sea 19 E4
Republic of South Africa
  21 B3
Reykjavík 26 B5
Rhône 28 C3
Rhine 26 C2

Riga 27 E3
Rio de Janeiro 14 D5
Rio Grande 8 B4
Riyadh 34 C3
Rocky Mountains 4 B4
Romania 29 D4
Rome 28 C3
Rosario 15 B4
Russian Federation 32 C3
Rwanda 20 C5

S

Sahara 18 C4
St George's Channel 25 B2
St Kitts and Nevis 9 F3
St Lawrence 5 E2
St Louis 7 D3
St Lucia 9 F2
St Petersburg 27 E3
St Vincent and the
  Grenadines 9 F2
Sakhalin 33 E3
Salvador 13 F1
Samoa 45 F4
San'a 34 C1
San Diego 6 A3
San Francisco 6 A3
San José 9 D2
San Juan 9 F3
San Marino 28 C3
San Salvador 8 C2
Santa Cruz 14 B6
Santiago 15 A4
Santo Domingo 9 E3
Santos 14 D5
São Francisco 13 F1
São Paulo 14 D5
São Tomé 18 C2
São Tomé and Principe 18 C2
Sapporo 39 E4
Sarajevo 29 D3
Sardinia 28 C3
Saudi Arabia 34 C2
Scotland 24 B5
Sea of Japan (East Sea)
  39 D4
Sea of Okhotsk 33 E3
Seattle 6 A5
Seine 26 C1
Senegal 18 B3
Seoul 39 D3
Serbia 29 D3
Seychelles 17 D4
Shanghai 39 D2
Shannon 25 A3
Sheffield 25 C3
Shetland Islands 24 C7
Siberia 32 C3
Sicily 28 C2
Sierra Leone 18 B2
Singapore 40 B3
Singapore 40 B3
Skopje 29 D3
Slovakia 29 D4
Slovenia 29 D4
Sofia 29 D3
Solomon Islands 45 D4
Solway Firth 25 C4
Somalia 20 D6

South America 10-11
Southampton 25 C1
South China Sea 38 C1
Southern Ocean 47
South Korea 39 D3
South Sudan 19 E2
Spain 28 A3
Sri Jayewardenepura Kotte
  37 C1
Sri Lanka 37 C1
Stockholm 27 D3
Stoke-on-Trent 25 C3
Strait of Gibraltar 28 A2
Sucre 14 B6
Sudan 19 E3
Suez Canal 19 E4
Sumatra 40 B2
Suriname 13 D3
Suva 45 E3
Swansea 25 C2
Swaziland 21 C3
Sweden 27 D3
Switzerland 28 C4
Sydney 44 C2
Syria 34 C4
Syrian Desert 34 C4

T

Tagus 28 A3
Taiwan 39 D1
Tajikistan 35 F4
Tallinn 27 E3
Tanzania 20 C5
Tashkent 35 F5
Tasman Sea 45 D1
Taurus Mountains 34 B4
T'bilisi 35 D5
Tegucigalpa 8 C2
Tehran 35 D4
Thailand 40 B4
Thar Desert 36 B4
The Bahamas 9 E4
The Gambia 18 B3
The Gulf 35 D3
The Hague 26 C2
The Pennines 25 C3
Thimphu 36 D5
Tien Shan 38 A4
Tierra del Fuego 15 B1
Timor Sea 44 A4
Tirana 29 D3
Tocantins 13 E1
Togo 18 C2
Tokyo 39 E3
Tonga 45 F3
Toronto 5 D1
Trent 25 D3
Trinidad and Tobago 9 F2
Tripoli 19 D4
Tunis 19 D5
Tunisia 18 C4
Turkey 34 C4
Turkmenistan 35 D4
Turks and Caicos Islands
  9 E3
Tuvalu 45 E4
Tyne 25 C4

U

Uganda 20 C6
Ukraine 29 E4
Ulan Bator 38 C4
Uluru (Ayers Rock) 44 B3
United Arab Emirates 35 D2
United Kingdom 25 B4
United States of America
  6 B3
Ural Mountains 32 B3
Uruguay 15 C4
Uzbekistan 35 E5

V

Valletta 29 D2
Vancouver 4 B2
Vanuatu 45 D4
Venezuela 12 C4
Victoria Falls 21 C4
Vienna 29 D4
Vientiane 40 B5
Vietnam 40 B4
Vilnius 27 E2
Vistula 27 D2
Vladivostok 33 E2
Volgograd 32 A3

W

Wales 25 C2
Warsaw 27 D2
Washington D.C. 7 E3
Wellington 45 E1
Western Ghats 37 B3
Western Sahara 18 B4
Windhoek 21 B3
Winnipeg 4 C2
Wrangel Island 33 E5

X

Xi'an 38 C3

Y

Yamoussoukro 18 B2
Yangon (Rangoon) 40 A4
Yaoundé 19 D2
Yaren 45 D5
Yekaterinburg 32 B3
Yellow Sea 39 D3
Yemen 34 C1
Yenisey 32 C3
Yerevan 34 C5
York 25 C3
Yucatán 8 C3
Yukon 4 B4

Z

Zagreb 29 D4
Zagros Mountains 35 D3
Zambezi 21 C4
Zambia 20 B4
Zimbabwe 21 C4

Answers

	Try this!		What am I?
2-3	GREENLAND		
4-5	1. Canadian goose, Arctic tern, snowy owl, snow goose, ptarmigan		A maple leaf
	2. Newfoundland, husky		
	3. polar bear, musk ox, Arctic fox, wolf, brown bear, bobcat, caribou, moose, beaver, Arctic hare		
6-7	1. blueberries, grapes, oranges, apples		A hot dog
	2. hotdog, hamburger, muffin		
	3. peanut		
8-9	1. tropical fish, sea horse, great white shark, elephant seal, monk seal, turtle		A cactus
	2. parrot, toucan		
10-11	1. Colombia, Chile	2. Bogota, Brasilia	
12-13	1. emerald, diamond	2. anaconda	A condor
14-15	1. mackerel, sardine		A killer whale
	2. polo, skiing, football, motor racing		
16-17	MADAGASCAR		
18-19	1. camel, gerbil, baboon		A camel
	2. scorpion, tortoise		
	3. hoopoe, hornbill bird, bee eater bird, secretary bird		
20-21	1. grapes, oranges	2. cloves	A sand dune
22-23	1. Two. Germany and Belgium		
	2. Greece	3. Norway	
24-25	1. football, cricket, rugby		A shamrock
	2. yachting, windsurfing		
	3. curling, skiing		
26-27	1. Gouda	2. dairy cows, pigs, sheep	An owl
	3. croissant		
28-29			Spaghetti
30-31	Sri Lanka		
32-33	1. reindeer, polar bear, Siberian tiger, Siberian husky, Siberian stag, brown bear, lynx, Caspian seal, lemming		A brown bear
	2. eider duck, snow goose, Ural owl		
34-35	1. Arabian camel, Arabian fox, Arabian horse		A flamingo
	2. Mosque	3. cricket	
36-37	1. tiger, snow leopard, Asiatic lion		An octopus
	2. peacock, parakeet	3. Indian porcupine	
38-39	1. Giant panda		A terracotta soldier
	2. karate, sumo wrestling, skiing		
40-41	1. surfing and scuba diving		A Komodo dragon
42-43	FIJI AUSTRALIA NAURU		
44-45	1. black swan		A kangaroo
	2. sea horses, sperm whale, barracuda, flying fish, clown fish, great white shark, swordfish, octopus		
46	1. ski plane	2. kayak	
	3. snowmobile		
47			A penguin

63

Answers

56-57 Games and quizzes

Name the continents
1. North America
2. Europe
3. Asia
4. South America
5. Africa
6. Oceania
7. Antarctica

Name the countries
1. United States of America
2. Italy
3. Australia
4. Brazil
5. Thailand
6. France

Search for cities

A	O	W	E	L	L	I	N	G	T	O	N
B	P	X	Z	P	O	J	X	Z	Q	J	O
W	A	S	H	I	N	G	T	O	N	V	T
X	R	K	Y	Y	D	W	V	J	F	X	T
C	I	K	P	F	O	X	Z	Q	J	F	A
A	S	Z	B	A	N	G	K	O	K	X	W
N	J	V	Q	Z	X	X	C	H	Z	Y	A
B	R	A	S	I	L	I	A	W	X	T	V
E	W	H	G	M	X	Z	I	Z	F	U	X
R	O	M	E	X	Q	V	R	J	Q	N	F
R	V	W	T	O	K	Y	O	V	W	I	Q
A	Q	W	H	G	M	X	T	J	V	S	Q

Quiz 1
1. Russian Federation
2. Paris
3. 5 stars

Colour match
1. purple finch
2. pink flamingo
3. brown bear
4. blueberries
5. great white shark

Unscramble the countries
1. Japan
2. Italy
3. France
4. Mexico
5. India
6. Sudan

Quiz 2
1. River Nile
2. 3 (green, white and red)
3. Polar bears

Whose flag is this?
1. Canada
2. Australia
3. Greece
4. United States of America
5. Pakistan
6. Sweden
7. Brazil
8. Kenya
9. China
10. United Kingdom
11. New Zealand
12. Japan
13. Nepal
14. Chile
15. Republic of South Africa
16. Somalia

58-59 Games and quizzes

Name the oceans
1. Pacific Ocean
2. Atlantic Ocean
3. Indian Ocean
4. Arctic Ocean
5. Southern Ocean

Name the symbol
1. Puffin
2. Kiwi fruit
3. Walrus
4. Sydney Opera House
5. Cricket
6. Stonehenge

Quiz 3
1. Buenos Aires
2. 2
3. Japan

Symbol match
1. United Kingdom
2. France
3. United States of America
4. India
5. Australia
6. Swaziland

Which continent are you in?
1. Europe
2. Africa
3. North America
4. Asia
5. Oceania
6. South America

Search for countries

A	R	G	E	N	T	I	N	A	F	K	Y
N	V	G	F	Y	N	E	Z	U	Z	B	V
C	Y	D	Q	C	G	G	G	S	X	Q	J
H	U	N	G	A	R	Y	B	T	G	B	J
I	L	A	F	N	G	P	H	R	B	O	Q
N	N	L	Z	A	S	T	V	A	P	T	X
A	G	O	X	D	T	V	F	L	H	S	F
H	P	O	L	A	N	D	Z	I	H	W	F
H	Y	X	Q	Q	V	Z	X	A	Z	A	O
M	E	X	I	C	O	G	G	V	G	N	Q
Q	Z	J	B	Y	F	F	B	X	B	A	J
N	I	G	E	R	I	A	B	J	Q	K	P

Quiz 4
1. Mount Everest
2. Beijing
3. Australia